Secondary Break

An NBA Dad's Story

Marvin Williams Sr

Fulton Books, Inc.
Meadville, PA

Published by Fulton Books 2020

ISBN 978-1-64654-124-9 (paperback)
ISBN 978-1-64654-125-6 (digital)

Printed in the United States of America

In Memory of Bishop Lawrence Ray Robertson

ACKNOWLEDGMENT

First and foremost, I would like to thank God for his many blessings he has bestowed upon me. I know without his grace and mercy none of this would be possible. I'd also like to thank my mother Ellis Henry Williams and my dad Horace Bennerman Jr for teaching me to say thank you and please. Secondly, I would like to say thank you to Marjorie Waye and her company Savior Publishing, LLC, for helping me to get this project started. Third, I want to thank Jim Tanner and his company Tandem Sports and Entertainment for all the years of love and support they have given to me and my family. Fourth, I'd like to give thanks to Bishop Lawrence Robertson for always encouraging me to be the best person I could be and for teaching me that if you can dream it you can achieve it. Fifthly, I would love to thank my family, Harvey, Jeffrey, Bradford, Terry, Arenda and Tavarish for all the years of love and support. Finally, but not least I'd like to thank Megan Mcgowan at Fulton Books for all of her patience and support throughout this process.

AUTHOR'S NOTE

This book is a work of nonfiction. I have recorded the events faithfully and honestly just as I remembered them. To anyone whose name I did not mention or recall, I offer sincere apologies. While circumstances and conversations depicted herein come from my keen recollection of them, they are not meant to represent precise timelines of events or exact word for word reenactments of my life. They are told in a way that evokes the real feelings and meaning of what was said and my view of what happened to me, in keeping with the true essence of mood and spirit of those moments that shaped my life.

Photo of author with his son

FOREWORD

I crossed paths with Marvin Williams, Sr. many years ago through his mother-in-law, Barbara Phillips. She is a member of the church I pastor and would bring his son and her grandson, Marvin Williams, Jr. to church with her as a youth. I also officiated his wedding to Andrea Gittens, Marvin Jr.'s mother. As I read this book, I reflected on watching Marvin Williams, Jr. play basketball with his friends growing up and imagined that it was with this same passion his father played as a youth in high school and in college. As the adage goes, "the apple doesn't fall far from the tree." Driven by the same desire for greatness as his father, Marvin Williams, Jr. grew up to become the second overall draft pick in the 2005 NBA draft and is currently a power forward with The Charlotte Hornets.

Marvin Williams, Sr. was raised in a time marred by racial inequalities and social injustices, a time where gangs were starting to become ubiquitous and a dismal future was almost certain. He was raised on a shaky foundation by alcoholic parents where the only reliable thing was instability. There were many paths he could go down growing up, but almost all of them were dubious forcing him to instead look within, fueled by passion and the hope of something better for himself and his family. It seems like basketball was the only constant in his life as every path he chose circled back to the sport. He has experienced the pinnacle of every parent's hopes and dreams, which is to see our children become a great success. His current life dwarfs his modest beginnings. Brought up in a family of sharecroppers, he now rubs arms with the NBA's elite. Marvin had to wrestle with the disappointment of not realizing his own dreams of becoming an NBA star only to realize that sometimes our dreams are fulfilled through our offspring creating a legacy for future generations, and that is not a disappointment at all.

Marvin Williams, Sr. is a remarkable man whose unrelenting support of his son is beautifully complemented by his humility. Words like tenacity, resiliency and driven come to mind when I think of him. His story is one of triumph and proves it doesn't matter how you start, only how you finish. He uses his platform to uplift others through his motivational speaking and philanthropic endeavors. This book is a must read for anyone who has ever faced adversity or the disheartening experience of a dashed dream. In concert with the theme of this book, our lives are ultimately like a basketball team. There are many players, and some are on our team and some on the opposing side. There are crowds in the stands cheering us on and others hoping for our demise. This book is a reminder that regardless of what the world thinks of you, it is God's thoughts of us that ultimately prevail. We just have to keep going, keep trying and keep believing.

Bishop Lawrence Robertson
Senior Pastor, Emmanuel Apostolic Church
President, New Life Community Development
Agency—Home of the Marvin Williams Center

INTRODUCTION

Four seconds! Run it down. Set it up. Point got it. He's taking his time, bringing it down and surveying the court. He's covered tight, and they're matched up perfectly. They're both six feet one inch, they are both quick, and they both have a laser-like focus on what's going on everywhere, even behind them. They are in man-to-man coverage and the point guard is covered. I break away to the top of the key, and he lobs it to me. Four seconds. That's all. That is the only thing that is important. I can't worry about my family and what they need. I can't think about how my back hurt after that hard work out and practice last night. I can't think about my need for breath as my chest heaves to gain the necessary air to live, or how nervous I am before this set began that made me feel like I wouldn't have the strength to play. All I have are these four seconds!

Three seconds. I turn to my left with wide legs almost in a squat as I catch it. I'm at the top of the key, and because I have it, I see the bodies, shifting in my direction. They are moving away from me, and in a split second, I have to change their momentum to keep them from reaching me before I extend myself and release it. The shift in the momentum of my adversaries coming at me increases my need to breath, my need to focus, and my need to complete my task. Will I succeed? The seconds are ticking away.

Two seconds. I'm bringing my feet together before I spring into the air. All the force I generated, now climbing up my body into my arms that are holding it. The energy, now reaching the tips of my fingers. All other moments in my life have led to this moment. These two seconds are all that I have. As I send it propelling off the tips of my fingers into the air toward the rim, I have put it all out there. I have put all of my mind, body, and soul into its propulsion. I can't do anymore. I have put all I have into this shot.

One second. It is now flying in the direction of the circle of my life! The circle is my enemy and my friend. It is my confidant and my adversary. The circle has brought me my greatest triumphs and my most difficult defeats. I trust the circle enough to know when it takes my side and when it will reject me with all of its force.

Swish! Today is my day. Today, this moment I lay bare, the vulnerable me, because all I gave comes back full circle.

We are fortunate. We who have found a place to exert our passions. We who intentionally accept the journey of life represented within our passions. Have you ever taken the time to look at that one thing you love and notice how it seems to mirror your life? In your passions, you have laughed and cried. You have prayed and you have sacrificed. In your passions, you have had to wait for its acceptance, and you have seen your innermost insecurities surface time and time again. In your passions, you have seen your kids also grow and develop even when they did or did not follow in your footsteps and share your same pathway. This is a story about how, in my passion, I have been able to see God, life, love, and a journey that lives on in the seeds I have planted along the way.

Every step of my life has mirrored that four-second play. That is what our lives consist of: seconds! We make split-second decisions that affect not only our lives, but the lives of everyone we touch. We decide if we want to eat healthy or not-so healthy. We decide in seconds if we are going to commit our lives to that one person or another. We decide if we are going to take a chance and do something that is scary, like trying something we have failed at before.

Seconds are all we have. Then we have to live with, or reconcile the consequences of those split-second decisions. None of us get to choose how we make it inside this human existence. However, there is a point in all our lives that we not only get to choose but, also get to decide, which lane we are going to run in.

From a very young age, I grew content with my split-second decision to choose to live instead of letting life choose for me. I didn't always understand that was what I was doing. But when I look back at the choices I have made, some great and some very, very bad, I can see I was making split-second decision about the lane I would take for my life. Every step of the way, I chose my passions and did my best to pour the lessons, of what those split-second decisions to live my passions have taught me, into the lives I have been blessed to touch.

CHAPTER 1

New York, 1964. I was born Marvin Gaye Williams, one of the eight children to my parents. It's been said that the sixties was the best time in Black-American history, and in a lot of ways, it's not difficult to see why that's not too much of a stretch, especially when you have today to compare it with. Think about it. The sixties gave black folks *leadership*. The kind of leadership we still talk about today. Hell, the kind of leadership that resulted in national holidays and a new way to see our own value as a black person in America. Malcolm X, Martin Luther King Jr.,

Muhammad Ali, and the Black Panthers. These are the legends that I remember growing up with and the names that filled the house, the streets, and the shape of our lives and struggles.

In a lot of ways, my first home set the pattern for many of my earliest struggles and achievements, to say nothing of the underlying sense of how life was back then. I grew up on Legion Street in Brooklyn, right down the road from our school, P.S. 156. We lived in a Brownstone. Our brownstone was three stories high, and every family knew one another. There were apartments on each floor within our brownstone community. There were eight of us living in our brownstone apartment in the back on the first floor: Mom; my brothers Harvey, Jeffrey, and Bradford; the baby; me; and my sister, Theresa. My dad worked in Long Island, doing his cooking show for a nice Jewish man, but would come home on the weekends.

The other families in our brownstone community included the Muslim family on the first floor. I went to school with their kids. on Sundays, I would sometimes go with them into the Harlem mosque where we would all sit together in one big room, all on the floor, no chairs or nothing, listening together to the message from a single jukebox. The single jukebox sat at the front of the mosque on an empty table. The jukebox, positioned like a pastor in other churches, was the only voice in the room. The message of Elijah Muhammed was delivered by notable persons like Malcolm X.

I remember running down to the Muslim family's home when I needed to get away from my own family's craziness. I was young but inquisitive (black folks would call me "Nosey"), and I loved interacting with people. I remember loving to learn in school and also from people whose lives appeared different than mine. That's what struck me about the Muslim family. Their family was different than mine, and they always let me come over and stay awhile. I remember I got my first ear piercing from a Muslim woman when I was just eight years old.

Another neighbor was a karate teacher I called Mr. Kelly, and I remember being impressed as all hell with his abilities. It was so cool to know that he studied under and trained with Chuck Norris. My father once asked him to train my brother and me in karate. We would visit our new karate teacher and learn some techniques. I just remember it being fun to play with all of his equipment, or toys as I saw them.

Living on Legion Street was a time where everyone was allowed to be in everyone else's business because it helped everyone stay safe. If a kid was in the middle of the street, acting a fool, any neighborhood parent could come out and pull them by the ear, pop them with a switch they just grabbed off of the closest tree, and then take the kid to their parent, grandparent, aunt, or uncle to report they were being bad. Every kid on the block knew if a neighbor witnessed them being bad out on the street and brought them to their family, the punishment they had coming from their family would be twice the pain. They would get their ass beat once because they did something bad and the second time because they embarrassed the family. Kids knew they were better off being good, or at least acting that way. The communities embraced each other, protected each other, watched out for each other because typically, everyone was in the same or similar situation. Families with working or trying-to-work parents just trying to survive. For better or worse, some of the best lessons of my life went hand in hand with the hardness.

The community was real back then. Every Sunday, like clockwork, the whole family would come out to gather on the stoop, like a family reunion. This family reunion took place not just with our family but with most of the families in our communities. For me, it was my mom and dad; brothers; sister; cousins Madeline and Marie; aunts Pearl, Mary, and Thelma; and also my uncles Rudy, sometimes Kirby Lee who lived in Philadelphia, Pennsylvania. It always felt like we had enough food to feed the whole block. All of the food that makes a black family gather again and again: macaroni and cheese, ham, greens, baked beans, cornbread, and more all cooked to perfection with every cake and pie imaginable available as well.

One of my favorite memories about the place, and one that really defined how the classic Brooklyn brownstone neighborhoods worked, was what I like to remember as the great pigeon wars. See, every building (or most of them) had open rooftops, and most rooftops had a pigeon coop. Flying pigeon became our thing, something to make our dad proud. It worked like this. My father would go and buy us, say, half a dozen homing pigeons, and we'd keep them in the coop for a while to get them used to us and their color. The key here was color. Our coop would be painted a bright blue. A building two streets away might have one bright red inside and out. The birds would then associate their color to their home flock. Then this is where it got fun because you would keep an eye out for when your neighbor let his birds out to fly. We would jump up and let out our flock when theirs got close and let the birds mix, then whistle for them to come home. If your birds were smarter than theirs, then they'd pull the whole mixed flock back to your coop, and suddenly, you've got all the birds, or you lost them all to smarter birds and a sharper whistle.

Where the current New York Nets arena sits used to be a market where they sold live pigeons. My dad bought about ten pigeons. We had them for a couple months, training them to recognize our blue coop. There was a Puerto Rican guy with a corner store. His nephew would compete with his pigeons. During one competition, we lost all the pigeons to this guy, and my dad threatened us, saying it would be the last time he would buy us pigeons. It could have been our desperation or sheer luck, but the next time we competed with him, we took all sixty of his pigeons. My dad had to build us a larger coop. The Puerto Rican uncle approached my dad, asking for his birds back. My dad told the guy; "You know the rules. If we lost, you wouldn't give our birds back!"

I was surrounded by family. I had my mom and dad, my brothers and sister, my aunt Thelma lived in the next brownstone building, and my aunt Pearl lived with her husband, Rudy, not too far away from us. I went to school with my cousins Madeline and Marie, and My aunt Mary was always around to show us what Jesus had to say about whatever we were doing good or bad. Despite all the challenges in our lives, we had love. My parents were both major players in my life, but it took me a lifetime to be able to look back, as a grown man, at the lessons and dynamics that were fully in play. Black families have a long-standing tradition, be it good or bad, of not really opening up with each other. Rarely do you find adults in black families, sharing their past experience with relationships, abuse, mental disorders, family secrets, or anything. This means that as a kid, you see the end results of all decisions and issues but don't know their cause. My brothers, sisters, and I were then left in a bad spot a lot of the time, thinking all the troubles our parents were going through were somehow our fault.

My parents were together for forty-one years. They had all of us kids moved back and forth from North Carolina to New York and remained unmarried. Although it is painful to say, my parents were also alcoholics. I believe my parents loved each other and were somehow, in a crazy yet cool way, made for each other. The circumstances that resulted in them being unmarried, raising a family for forty-one years stems from some generational, cultural, and economic shit that was just what it was—the truth in the black community! The stuff that came from the hundreds of years of slavery in the South. Thousands of families ripped apart where fathers and mothers have children, then the mother or the father is ripped away from one plantation to other plantations where new families get started. Thousands of years where men and women had to be hard toward love and family. A hardness that numbed both men and women into believing that it's okay for men to have multiple families. A hardness that numbed my mother, or perhaps my father's wife, into accepting that my father had nineteen children and maintained two separate families.

My father was a strong man who struggled all his life, both with what life threw at him and also with his own decisions. My dad finished the sixth grade and never put much stock in books or any kind of education. But he was one of the smartest men I have ever known. He had a PhD in street smarts. If there was an angle, he could find it and make it work. If any man could be called a jack-of-all-trades, it was my daddy. He was a mechanic, a tank driver in the Army, a chef, a handyman, a baker, and just about everything else at some point in his life. Then of course, there was the television cooking show on Long Island, where my brothers and sister got to watch and be proud of our dad. Cooking was one thing that, I remember, he really loved, he took incredible pride in everything he did because he did it damn well.

My dad grew up in Chinquapin (Chinkapin), North Carolina. He grew up with a tough father, which in turn made him tough. When my dad was young, he grew up in a poor family. He used to talk about how hungry he was growing up. He and his five siblings would go to school and church in the same building. They were all in a one classroom church, like the one on Little House on the Prairie, just not like that because he was black. He talked about going to school and church where he would have to tighten his belt so much to stop the grumbling in his stomach. My father grew up in a time in the South where sharecropping, or just a step above sharecropping, was how his family cared for the kids. The slave mentality was alive and real as many of the men of the family had been slaves as children. The family worked for the white man and hope was a scarce thing.

I remember a story my father told me that summed up how hard my grandfather was on my father. It was about him and his brother, Kirby Lee. My grandfather, who I don't remember meeting, would get drunk at night and fall asleep. My dad and uncle wanted to learn how to drive, so they would sneak out of the house when my grandfather fell asleep. They would steal the car, and with my father behind the wheel, my uncle would push the pickup truck down the dirt road so that they could practice driving. On one of their driving lessons, they drove the truck into a water well. Keep in mind, they only drove in the dark, and the only lights were those on the headlights of the pickup truck. When my grandfather found out and reached my father and uncle, no words were spoken, only screams and yelps from how badly Granddad beat both of them. I believe that between the beatings and the lack of physical affection, since neither my grandfather nor father believed in hugging or being touchy-feely, my father became tough as nails.

My father's family was very interesting. My aunt Katie was the youngest worked for Macy's in New York for over twenty years. I remember going to all the Macy's Christmas and Thanksgiving parades with her. She was a very beautiful woman whom I spent a lot of my young life with. Her husband, Rudy, was also an amazing (but very strange) man. He was a plumber by trade and taught me a lot of valuable lessons growing up. He taught me the value of love and hard work, and my weekends with him were always exciting. There were times we would be working in dark and smelly basements, fixing people's pipes. Aunt Pearl and Uncle Rudy had a great love for dogs. The bad part about living with them was that I had to clean out the room where all the dogs were kept. Nearly every day after school, Aunt Pearl would come get me from Legion Street, and I would spend the week (or weekend) with them. I would be responsible for taking up the used filthy newspapers and putting down a fresh layer for the dogs. In return, she would pay me some pocket money, though I remember Uncle Rudy believed that if I ate his food and slept in his house, taking care of the dogs was my fair payment in return for spending the night and feeding me.

My dad also had another sister, Aunt Mary, who lived in the city. We all lived close to each other. Aunt Mary was very religious, so when she would come around to visit, all of the family would stop their drinking and gambling because if you didn't, she would give you an earful of God's word. My dad also had an older brother, Kirby Lee, who lived in Philadelphia, Pennsylvania. He would hardly come around, but when he did, all of us kids knew that something in the family had gone wrong and that he was there to straighten it out. Uncle Kirby Lee wasn't a loud man. In fact, as a kid, I barely heard him speak. He wasn't a loud boastful man. He was the guy that when he came to talk, you knew something was wrong. I loved him because he was so unlike my dad—a forward thinker. He would always come by during the summer to try to get my dad to take us somewhere fun (like Las Vegas or Disneyland), but my dad would never do it. My dad believed in hard work and buying us the things he thought we needed and the things he wanted us to learn from, like the pigeons, or the musical instruments. My mom, on the other hand, was very adventurous. She believed in trying anything and felt like we (as kids) should get to see the world.

My mother's family was from the Deep South, and we would go to North Carolina some summers to see our granddad and grandma. The Deep South in the summer, unlike New York, was extra hot, had lots of dirt roads, and outhouses. Outhouses, meaning that if you had to go to the bathroom, you could not go in the house. You had to go outside of your house to go to the bathroom. Deep South North Carolina also had tobacco fields. My mother's family did not own the tobacco fields, but when we visited our grandparents, they would immediately dispatch us to the fields to start cropping. Tobacco was big business in the area with major companies like R. J. Reynolds and Marlboro cigarettes. We went from being city kids to Deep South farmers with a single car ride.

The stench of segregation, racism, and hatred was everywhere in the South. I despised the attitudes and the tension created every time we were around white people. Even as a kid, I understood the sheer hatred of white people anytime a black person was present. It wasn't because it was something that white people said, it was because their hatred came through in everything they said to black people and every action they made around us. During that time, white folks felt like black folks were not equal to them and that our only place was in the tobacco fields. We spent a lot of time, going back and forth to the South. I remember as a kid, reading Jet magazine while riding in the car on our way down South.

Jet magazine was the premier weekly magazine, highlighting stories about black people from all walks of life. This magazine show-cased the good, the bad, and the ugly of the plight of the black person. I remember seeing a picture of a young black soldier, hanging from a tree in Georgia. The US military soldier had come home for two weeks to visit his family. He was then taken by some members of the Klu Klux Klan, a white racist hate group, and hung from a tree. This photo had such a major impact on my life that the image still sticks with me to this day. Racism was a part of our culture in New York as well but not as open and cruel as it was in the South. In New York, we all seemed to manage to get along with our neighbors regardless of the other person's race because New York was one big melting pot.

My grandparents were extremely poor, and just like using the outhouse to go to the bathroom, we also had to bathe in a metal tub outside in the yard at night because they had no indoor plumbing.

There was a bright spot in going to North Carolina during the summertime. When us kids weren't out cropping tobacco leaves, I loved going to the countryside. On the countryside, there were wide open fields of land that I could play on. My family would stay with our grandparents for about a month during the summertime, soak up the sun, build lots of muscles from cropping tobacco all day, and conquer any possible fears we may have had from having to venture out to the outhouse after dark. At the end of the month, we would all climb in the car and travel back to the natural city life of New York. I remember this routine, summer in and summer out, until I was ten years old.

CHAPTER 2

New York, 1971. I was seven years old and was getting a real taste of real life. When I was seven, I learned all about gang life, the real meaning of friendship, and the definition of poverty. I also learned about how to lean on family, the reality of being black in a world where the Black Panthers existed, and an introduction into what would become my lifelong passions. You don't really know something is going to steal your heart until you give your heart to it. In a split-second decision, I would learn what planting a seed into someone's life would mean.

Now there was never a time when New York didn't have issues, but they were different back then. Gangs, for instance, were a whole different thing. Today's gang mess is just horrible all the way around. Back then, it at least seemed there was a "code", a purpose beyond just being feared and proving you were harder than the next fool. Don't get me wrong, territory was still an issue. Each gang would lay claim to their blocks and defend them, but not with guns and random shootings. The innocent kid getting shot down through his or her bedroom window was unheard of, unimaginable.

Gangs were about territory. You and your group claimed an area of the streets. This micro community was controlled or managed by the gang leaders. Like a corporation, gangs had hierarchies like a CEO, an operation manager or COO, management, and then the workers. Everyone in the gang corporation had a job to do and a central purpose: protect our turf, our area, our corporation at any cost. The gang corporation also had a family aspect. Members of the gangs were generally folks in the area of the territory that either had no family or had family that did not care for them. You could always get love and respect while also learning about life from the gang's perspective, from the gang corporation.

Two of my best friends in elementary school, Tony and Montgomery, both had uncles who were in gangs. The challenge to the gang corporation idea was that the folks in the gangs still lived in the projects and were still super poor. One of the major gangs in Brooklyn were in the projects that Jay-Z grew up in, the Marcy Projects. The members of the gangs and those they protected, still had to hustle and scrape for the basics of life. I remember visiting Tony's house one day when his uncle wasn't at home. I went over there with my dad because as a community, if we saw a problem with anyone, we would step in and help where we could. I remember my dad, asking Tony about his uncle, when was the last time he saw him, and if he had food to eat. Tony told my dad that he had food and that he was all right. I think we were both about six or seven years old at that time. I went into Tony's kitchen to check on how much food he had. I opened the kitchen cabinets, and all I saw were cans and cans, stacked as high as the cabinet, of ALPO chunky dog food. No beans or soup, no rice or bread, no milk or butter in the refrigerator, just dog food, and Tony didn't have a dog.

I learned that day what poor really meant. I understood how bad it was for people. You hustle or work a job. You are just barely getting by, and still, the best you can do is feed the kids you are responsible for dog food. This was real poverty.

Today, when I look back at how the Black Panther Party was portrayed as a gang, or a domestic terrorist group, it pisses me off. The Black Panther Party in reality was neither a gang, nor a terrorist group. They were simply a group that saw issues in the black community that the government couldn't understand and wouldn't contribute funds to correct. Instead of waiting for someone else to fix things, the Black Panthers created solutions. The Black Panther Party that I saw provided resources, information, and programs for underprivileged communities. In my community, the Black Panther Party fought for kids to have summer lunch programs in every community. They were not concerned about race when it came to the underprivileged, except for the fact that most of the underprivileged kids in the communities I knew about were the black kids.

The Black Panther Party also used the strength and intelligence of the members of the party to fight injustices. There was a case in my neighborhood where an elderly white lady caused a riot. When you walked out on the stoop, you could almost taste the smoke from the ashes of the fire that were set some time overnight. When walking to the corner store, it was not surprising to see a massive city bus overturned on the streets. We could hear the clang of metal from chains or crowbars, connecting from the fighting that took place overnight outside our windows. The violence every night, a reaction to the frustration, anger, and outrage of people over the civil injustices, again against the mostly black communities. My parents were afraid for us kids, just walking down our street to the corner store because anything could happen to us from the time we stepped on the stoop and down the stairs outside of the brownstone just trying to get to the store to buy whatever until we got back home.

A teenage black kid that the elderly lady knew from the neighborhood was just trying to make some extra cash. He asked his neighbors for work tasks and odd jobs that he could do for money. One of his customers was this elderly white lady who needed her basement cleaned up. She was elderly, her husband had passed away, and she was unable to clean up the junk in her basement by herself. The young man and the elderly woman came to an agreement that she would pay him for coming over to her house after school to clean and organize her basement. Since the elderly woman had troubles getting down her stairs, she told the young man that he didn't have to come to her front door to access the basement but, instead, let himself into the basement after school by taking the stairs on the side of the house.

The boy came to the elderly woman's home within the next couple of days and did as he was told. He took the stairs on the side of the elderly woman's home down to the basement to let himself in. Unknown to the young man, the elderly woman became frightened by the noises, coming from her basement area and thought there must be a burglar, attempting to get into her home. The elderly woman called the police and told them someone was trying to break into her home by the basement. When the police arrived, they found the young man downstairs in the basement holding a broom. They didn't ask him what he was doing down there. They shot the boy dead with the broom still in his hand. Them Jokers didn't give him a chance to explain or try to arrest him by giving him a chance to put the broom down. They didn't yell, "Put your hands up!" They saw a black boy in a white lady's basement and, without remorse, shot him dead.

The city was in an uproar over this incident, mostly because everyone in the neighborhood knew the elderly woman gave the young man permission to work in her basement. The parents of the young man discussed the agreement with the elderly woman and gave their blessing for this young man to work for the elderly woman. The police department was so corrupt, even when the elderly lady came forward and admitted she forgot she gave the young man permission to work in her basement. They tried to simply ignore the situation. For more than a week, there were riots within the city. Buses were overturned, people were getting shot and killed. Emotions were running high while hope for a time of justice for the black community was damn near dead. That was until the Black Panther Party got involved. The Black Panther Party demanded and subsequently succeeded in getting this woman arrested for her part in the killing of an innocent black male. To the elderly woman's credit, her personal guilt made her admit her wrongdoing. However, without the intervention of the Black Panther Party, this injustice would have been swept under the rug.

There are numerous stories about black people, especially black men, being harassed by police. I wish I could say times have changed since the sixties and seventies, but unfortunately, this is the shit that makes black people and real human beings disgusted with the police and the abuse of power. This is the shit that makes you sick to your stomach but also become hardened to the idea that this reality for so many. This is the shit that makes you shake your head, knowing it ain't right, but this is the fight every day. The fight against the attack on black communities that continues today. It is like a stain on your favorite shirt. Try as you might, it never seems to go away. The difference today is that there aren't organizations like the Black Panthers on a national level who, with a unified national mission, step in to find solutions for anyone, experiencing the attacks of injustices we see today.

One of the greatest things I saw the Blank Panther Party organize was the summer lunch program. This program was available in every community around Brooklyn, and I believe they covered almost all of the neighborhoods in and around New York City. This summer lunch program was so important to me because I believe my friend Montgomery would have died without it. Montgomery was one of my close friends who, like Tony, was severely poor. Montgomery used to come to school with an ashy face. He looked like he just took a bath but had no lotion all of the time. Montgomery would go days, wearing the same clothing, and he never had any money. During the summer, we would take lunch breaks and head over to the corner store. My mom gave me money, and I would share it with Montgomery to make sure he could get something with me that he would share with his little brother and sister. When the summer lunch program started with the Black Panthers, Montgomery had the opportunity to feed himself, his brother, and his sister at least once a day.

Being friends with Montgomery became one of my split-second decisions. In fact, it turned out Montgomery was the start of the journey to my passion. I remember being six or seven years old, watching the older kids playing basketball before, during, and after school. It was cool to watch, but at that time, I was a nerd and had more fun competing with my cousin Madeline to see who could get the best grades in school. I loved learning new things, even at six or seven years old. However, one day, Tony asked me why I wasn't playing basketball with our friends. I told him I wasn't truly interested in the game even though it looked kind of fun. Tony pushed me to ask Montgomery to teach me how to play because he was really good. Finally, my split-second decision: I agreed to go and learn how to play basketball from Montgomery.

Montgomery was excited to teach me how to play, but how and where he would teach me would be very unique. Montgomery was the oldest child of his mother's as far as I knew. He had a younger brother and sister that he took care of. At six or seven years old, when school ended for the day, Montgomery had to go straight home to take care of his siblings. Seeing that Montgomery wore the same clothes every day and never had any lotion and barely had enough food to keep himself alive made seeing him go home and take care of two younger kids even worse. There was never any food in the house, so seeing him try to put something, anything together to care for them was just sad. We would practice playing basketball outside his house, close enough to make sure that if his brother and sister needed something, he was there to take care of them. I never saw Montgomery's mom Monday through Sunday. To this day, I have no idea what his mother even looks like. I used to stay at his house with him to try to help him out. Montgomery saw his situation as normal, just like Tony, because at such a young age, the way they lived was all they knew. All they knew was *p-o-v-e-r-t-y*!

Montgomery, despite his home situation, was a great basketball teacher. I learned to play basketball because it was fun, playing with him and Tony. He broke down basketball in a kid's way—the only way to learn is to do it. We would run drills, and I was learning while playing something he made fun. Montgomery and Tony would share the professional basketball teams and players they loved to watch play the game. Tony loved Clyde "the Glide," Walt Frazier, and the New York Knicks was our team. I'd take any chance I could get to watch them on TV, and I would go play every day after school.

I remember going home after playing all day to my parents' fighting each other all night. It would get so violent that we would have to go stay at my aunt's house for days on end. My parents would cut into each other, and both would be so drunk that they didn't care about us. When they got in their moods to fight, we spent a lot of time, looking out for the police on our street because the neighbors would call them on my parents. Their fights would get so loud and physical.

In 1971, Julius "Dr. J" Erving joined the American Basketball Association (ABA) to become the star player on the Virginia Squires professional basketball team. He couldn't get into the NBA because they had a rule at that time that in order to be drafted, you had to be out of high school at least four years. I began really focusing on basketball and watching Dr. J. play was like a dream I wanted for myself. Dr. J. was originally from New York, and he did some superhuman amazing things with the basketball. His hands were so big, he could hold a basketball in his hands like it was a tennis ball. This amazing basketball player became my idol, and I would follow his every move and career for the rest of my life.

To this day, I truly think that if it wasn't for Dr. J, I wouldn't have survived, coming up in New York. My friends, as they got older, began to get involved in more and more gang activities. There were so many gangs in New York. We had the warlords, the disciples, the young bloods, and the five percenters. There were female versions of each of these gangs as well. I remember walking out of school one day and seeing one girl gang, fighting another girl gang while the boys of one gang were fighting the other boys with chains. It was bloody and violent as hell. That was not the pathway for me. I could have decided to go the path of gang life. I mean, I was already running away from the violence in my own home. I could have easily gone the way of the gangs. Unlike my friends, my destiny and my seconds were happily hitched to basketball.

CHAPTER 3

With all the negative stuff going on in New York, there were some good things as well: I got to see Mick Jagger for free in Central Park on a school trip; I got to see Willis Reed return for the New York Knicks; and I got to spend a lot of time at the Brooklyn museum, which was my absolute favorite place. For a young kid in the seventies, New York was a great place to grow up. My family, like New York, was dynamic in good and bad ways, no different than all families. Families are stained with the effects of our ancestors' split-second decisions. Did we make the right decision in having these kids in a world we know does not embrace our kind of ethnic magic? Did we make the right decision to move to a place, any place where we took up roots? Each decision made from one generation affects the next generation. Pretty soon, we simply stop considering the decisions and just make them the best we can. All decisions have a consequence. It's just a matter of which direction it takes us.

New York, 1972. When my friends started getting more and more into gangs, my parents decided that it was time for us to move within Brooklyn from Legion Street to Flatbush and Rogers. Flatbush and Rogers Street was a little more peaceful and quieter, and we would now be closer to my mother's sister, Aunt Thelma. My mom and Aunt Thelma were partners in crime, starting from a very young age. Growing up together, my mother, who was a tough fighting woman would get into fights. Her sister, Thelma, was always there to help her in every way she needed to. I loved Aunt Thelma with all my heart. She had three kids of her own: a daughter named Jackie and two sons. Bobby was the oldest, Darnell was the youngest and the youngest son died. Bobby grew up and spent most of his life in and out of prison. Jackie grew up to be the glue of the family despite her challenges at a young age. Jackie dated one of the most notorious drug lords in New York City. A drug lord is a guy who is basically the CEO of his own drug organization, even though selling drugs is illegal. The drug lord had managers, employees (the drug dealers on the street), suppliers, and vendors. Jackie had a child with her drug lord boyfriend when she was only seventeen. Through the grace of God, covering her and her daughter, she is now an amazing woman who not only takes care of her mother she but also cares for her special-needs niece.

Although Flatbush and Rogers Street was only one hour away from Legion Street, it was a world apart for me. Moving to Flatbush and Rogers was a little different. We had to get to know people on our block all over again. It was on Flatbush where I met the twins, who like me, loved to just have fun. It was with the twins I learned how to play handball after school. I loved that game. Handball is an outside game similar to playing racquetball except you use your hand instead of a racket. Handball was a game that forced you to be quick, moving from side to side. Every day, we would play handball and then basketball, and it sounds crazy, but the two sports helped me get better at both. Every so often, my brother Harvey and I would go back to the old neighborhood on Legion Street so that we could play a few games with my friend Montgomery who was now playing basketball for the school team.

By the time we moved to Flatbush, my dad quit his television cooking show and got a job working at a car wash company. Now that he was working closer to home, I got to spend more time with him. When he came home now, he would turn on music that we all loved like Marvin Gaye, The Temptations, The Jackson 5, The Manhattans, and Aretha Franklin. The best collection of music my dad would play was his collection of Sam Cooke albums, which he collected over ten years.

It was also during this time in my life (I think I was about nine) that my dad shared a family secret with my brother and me. Dad told me and my brother Harvey that we had a special connection to the singers we were listening to. He told us that when we were younger, we actually got to see all of these acts in real life. That secret seemed unreal. I didn't remember experiencing the pure heart and soul of some of the greatest performers the world has ever seen. Dad told us his sister Pearl was a ticket taker at the World-Famous Apollo Theatre in Harlem. She would let my dad and us into the theater to see all of the shows.

That's how I got my name, Marvin Gaye Williams. My parents went to see Marvin Gaye at the Apollo, and my mother just happened to be pregnant with me. As the silky voice of Marvin Gaye was ringing through the theatre, lulling everyone into a hypnotic trance, my mother went into labor, and the inspiration for my name Marvin Gaye Williams was born.

Moving to Flatbush and Rogers Street was an adjustment, but since we still went to the same school, it wasn't all bad. New York had this voucher system and would give kids green passes to ride the city buses to school. The only problem was we were kids. We lose stuff all the time. Me, I lost my bus pass more than once, so my brother Harvey and my sister Theresa had to be creative in making sure we could all get to school or back home because our parents were not going to pay for us to get new bus passes every time we lost it, which happened to be a lot of the time. I remember once my sister got on the bus at one stop and then I would run down to the next bus stop. While the line of passengers was getting on the bus, my sister would hand me her pass out the window and then I would get on. When I climbed on the bus, I showed my voucher, like it was mine all the time, and we rode to school. The bus drivers got hip to that game and stopped us from doing that. After that, I started catching the back bumper of the bus to ride to school. I would put my feet on the bumper and put my hand on the gas tank cover. I did that for a while until my uncle, who was driving by, saw me on the back bumper of the bus and told my dad. My dad beat me like I stole something that time, and every time I lost my bus pass, which again was a lot, I just stopped telling him.

New York City was a temptation I couldn't resist, and from Brooklyn, I could easily catch the train to Manhattan with my bus voucher. No one on the train was going to ask me or anyone else why this kid was riding the train on a school day, so some days I would ditch school and catch the train to Manhattan. The only catch when I skipped school was that I had to be back to Brooklyn, in front of my school, by the time school got out so my mom and dad wouldn't know. Manhattan was nothing like Manhattan today. Manhattan back in the seventies was full of pimps and prostitutes. There were strip joints and peep shows where you could pay a quarter to see women peep parts of their bodies, sometimes all of their bodies, to customers, looking at them through a window. Nobody ran kids away, so we would sit on the fire hydrants and watch people come up from the subway and predict, which guys were going to go to strip club based on how they were walking and looking around. I always loved watching people.

Remember the catch! I had to make sure I made it home before school was out so I wouldn't get caught skipping school. Once I didn't make it back home from Manhattan until around 3:00 p.m. and school got out at 2:00 p.m. This day, of all days, my dad was waiting for me at the school.

I got in the car and immediately, my dad asked me, "Where was you at?"

I was always quick on my feet, so I responded, "I got out of school late."

Yeah, I know I went to school with my brother Harvey and sister Theresa, and we got out of school technically at the same time, but with all of the previous beatings for simply losing my bus pass, there was no way I was telling him, "I skipped school and went to Manhattan. Again!"

My dad didn't say another word until we got home. He got out of the car, and I followed him into the house. He let me put my bag down and took me off to talk with me by myself. My dad was tough, and I knew his silence was not going to be good for me. He finally said, "I know you're lying, but I ain't gonna beat you this time." It took everything in me not to smile and wipe the invisible sweat from my brow. But just when I thought I was good, he said, "But!" I hate that word because everything after that was always the start of something bad. I mean, something bad for me. My dad continued and said, "but if you ever lie to me again, I am going to kill you!" My dad was not one to play, or kid around with his words. I knew he would really kill me—his kid, his blood. He wouldn't have hesitated, so he had no more problems out of me after that.

When I was ten years old, my siblings and I spent many nights with my aunt Thelma in Brooklyn. Mom's dad became very ill, and when we were not traveling down and back to North Carolina to see about my granddad, my mom was drinking more heavily and couldn't attend to us kids. We would take the long drive down to my grandparents' home, spend a few weeks down there, and then drive back to Brooklyn. When school was back in session, Mom and Dad would make the trip, and us kids would stay with Aunt Thelma and go to school. I knew it was coming, the day when my parents would tell us we were moving down to North Carolina. For a kid who was used to the diverse, active concrete jungle called Brooklyn, I just knew I didn't want to move to the South.

CHAPTER 4

New York, June 1974. After several trips from New York to North Carolina, my parents decided to permanently move to Wallace, North Carolina. The strain of traveling back and forth was taking its toll on my parents' relationship to the point where they decided to separate. My dad helped my mom make the decision to take us, six kids, to live with her parents while my dad stayed in New York. He was only supposed to be there a couple of months, but their separation lasted more than a year. Packing up our things and moving in with our grandparents would prove to be a nightmare.

Shortly after my family, minus my dad, migrated to Wallace, North Carolina, my grandfather passed away from his illness. Watching a family member suffer from an illness at a young age is difficult as you are mourning for an important branch of your family tree. The family tree that offers you grounding and roots of love, protection, and guidance in their own special way. It was also difficult because from a very young age, I knew my grandmother couldn't stand any of my mother's children. Without my grandfather, we would no longer have a shield of protection from her. I don't know if she hated us because my mother was always a rebel, or just because we were from New York. I never got the chance to ask her what her reasons were. I just tried to stay out of her way while we were there.

My grandmother's house was jam-packed with folks when my mother moved back home. We lived in the house: my mom and six kids with my two aunts, my uncle from time to time, and my grandmother. My grandmother lived in a house that was actually owned by my aunt Thelma. When Aunt Thelma was younger, she was married and had two kids. One was Jim and the other was Brenda. One night, Aunt Thelma and her husband went out for a night on the town to a nightclub. While they were at the nightclub, a fight broke out, and her husband was shot to death. Her husband had built the house for his family, and when he died, he left the house to her. My aunt Thelma moved her parents into the house, my granddad and grandma, and then she moved to New York with my mom. The house became big momma's house with family moving in and moving out over time.

The crazy part of moving back to North Carolina with my grandparents, even though the house was owned by Thelma, was that my grandmother treated all of us, including Aunt Thelma, like second-class citizens. I think she treated Thelma that way, when she visited home, because she always defended my mother, whom my grandmother obviously hated. We also got treated like second-class citizens when my second oldest sister Sandra, who had been taken care of since birth by my mom's sister Mary, came home from Charlotte with my other cousins. My grandmother treated them like upper class and us like scrubs when Sandra and my other cousins were there. They were definitely her favorites.

In North Carolina, we were enrolled in Wallace Elementary School. The schoolhouse was actually a small church. Fortunately for us, and without stating the obvious, it was time for a new school, which the community decided to build a year after we made Wallace, North Carolina our home. The new school was much bigger, and everything was new and improved. The school housed students between sixth and eighth grade. The only thing that was not new and improved was the way they disciplined the students when we misbehaved. This was the seventies, a time when there were no outlet covers to protect kids from electrocuting themselves. Kids could ride bikes without a helmet and paddling kids at school was an everyday occurrence. As much as I got paddled, you would have thought, *Damn! They must have been waiting for me to be a student there because I got it all the time, and it seemed no one else but me and my friends was getting.* This is not to say that my brother, me, and my new friends didn't misbehave, but the teachers never missed a chance to get at me. In order for a teacher to paddle you, they had to call an adult from your family to come and witness the punishment. My grandmother, who couldn't stand any of my mother's children and happened to be the closest to the school, wouldn't miss a chance to witness the embarrassing event. Did I say she wouldn't miss a chance? She was at *every* paddling, then she would later come home and tell everyone in the house that her grandson from New York is acting a fool and embarrassing the family. That was like telling the family and neighborhood, "Get him!"

So when the grandmother got word, "Hey, your grandson was acting up in school," then my uncle would come and say, "I heard you were acting up in school," followed by my aunts and, of course, the whole community. If you acted up in school, you would have a lineup of aunts who would now take turns paddling you for embarrassing the family at school. I'll never forget I got a beating from 6:00 p.m. to 11:00 p.m. one night. My uncle was so cold that he would take you out on a dirt road and give you like three car lengths. He would tell us if we could outrun him before he got to that highway, he would leave us alone. In the meantime, he said, "I'm going to stretch this belt out, and when I say run, you better run." He didn't care if he hit us across the head. We just kept running, and he kept swinging. By the time we got to the end of the dirt road, we didn't have any more issues with him. Of course, the neighbors would hear and call me out. "Come here, Marvin, I want you to do something for me." I go over to them, and I'm thinking I am going to do something to help them, but the neighbor would get me in the back room, shut the door, and give me the paddle. She would say, "I heard you was embarrassing your grandmother!" then she would start wailing on me.

Those were the boundaries, you're black and you don't embarrass yourself in front of the white folks. That is what you were raised on. Rule no. 1: don't embarrass your family in front of the white folks.

The white folks already think there is something wrong with you. Then your grandmother has built a good reputation, and now, I got my grandkids, coming down from New York, embarrassing me. They act like they weren't raised right, but to white folks, you're doing exactly what they expected.

God was huge. Everything. Part of the transition of moving to North Carolina from New York was that I ended up going to church seven days a week. In New York, I never thought about church. My mom grew up in the Bible belt but refused to push that on her kids.

Black folks in the south during the seventies was a very proud bunch. They believed in Jesus, so we went to Church! We went to church every day (sometimes we would go to church every night too) and Sundays, too, which was an all-day affair. Sundays were pretty much the only day we had off from cropping tobacco, which made sense why we spent the entire day at church, thanking Jesus for our blessings but also praying we lived to see the next Sunday, depending on what happened during the week. Life could change in seconds, and Jesus was our refuge and protection to make it through.

I remember there was a lady we called her Ms. Chiney. Her real name was Chiney Mae Dixon. She had this big old bell,, and she would ring it three times a day. Summertime or during school, she would still do the same thing every day. So she would ring the bell, and the grownups would tell the kids, "When you hear the bell, you better get up there." We all went up to her house and then she would pray. She would pray, pray over you, and read the word to us. This went on for about thirty minutes each time. If you acted up, you would get the stick. She would also make you attend. She would take kids in her station wagon to Clinton, North Carolina, which was about forty-five miles from where we lived. Every night during the summer, she made bread. She would smash the bread. It was the best-tasting bread I have ever eaten. I think she knew how to make the same bread Jesus had back in the day.

She was a really big influence on us kids. She always cared about the kids. She had ice cream she would give to the kids. She would make her own ice cream, cakes, and candies that she would sell to the kids. She was like the matriarch of the whole community. She was probably sixty at that time. When she said jump, you jumped, and all of the adults, my grandmother included, knew it. She was the pastor of the church, and when she said jump, you just did it.

41

We used the go to church at nine in the morning, and my grandmother would make a basket, even though we lived within walking distance to the church. It was about twenty minutes away. You went to Sunday school from 9:00 a.m. to 11:00 a.m., to church from 11:00 a.m. to 2:00 p.m., you stopped and had your lunch, and then you go back at night. Now you never left the church on Sunday. Me and my cousin William Newkirk would get restless, and we would sneak out and go up the street. The deacon would always catch us and bring us back in front of the whole church. In front of the whole congregation, the deacon used to have us stand up and say, "Whose kids are these?" And my mom and William's mom would have to stand up to claim us. They would be so embarrassed. The deacon would stop and bend us over right in front of the church. The deacon would make it seem like you didn't raise your children right, and he would spank us in front of the entire church. Then we would endure the same lineup of getting our asses beat from our family, no different than getting a paddling at school. There was always an opportunity to get your ass beat as a kid.

From the time we were thirteen to about seventeen years old, we had to go to church. Even when we didn't live with my grandmother, my mother still made us go to church. My grandmother would come over and get you if you didn't come to church. It helped build great character, and because of the foundation, you had something to turn to. When times got hard, throughout my life, all that I learned during that time, I always had God to turn to because God gave us Ms. Chiney.

It was one thing to crop tobacco during the summertime when we visited from New York, but now, Wallace, North Carolina, was our home. This meant that picking tobacco, or cropping tobacco as it was formally called, was part of our daily lives. We got up at 5:00 a.m. every day to get out to the tobacco fields and work late into the evening. Everyone from my mom and all of my aunts along with all us kids would be out there every day like this during the summers and get a pack of crackers and Coke for the day. As the word cropping implies, like sharecropping, we wouldn't get paid a lot for working all day, and on top of that, our parents would receive our earnings and use it how they saw fit to help us live. I know it's hard to compare it to slavery since there were some earnings going on, but for us kids, it was slavery. We worked from sunup to sundown, and we never touched a penny of the earnings made on our time, working that hard. Plus, we only got fed crackers and a Coke. What else can I say? That is slavery.

With all of that work, whenever we had any free time, I focused on my passion—playing basketball. It helped me escape from the fact that my grandmother hated us and would go out of her way to make sure we all knew it whenever we were around. It helped me escape from seeing my mother drown her feelings in a bottle of alcohol. Basketball was everything, and I was lucky because there were people around me who inspired me and took up time with me and my brother to make us better.

Our grandparents had one television set, and all we were able to watch was UNC basketball and the Miami Dolphins. Carolina had a young man on their team named Phil Ford, who was a local star from Rocky Mountain, North Carolina. While at the University of North Carolina, Ford averaged 18 points a game, won a gold medal on the US Olympic basketball team in 1976, and finished his college career as the all-time leading scorers in the school's history. Phil Ford was an unselfish player with the greatest work ethic and basketball IQ. We would watch him play every weekend like it was a religion. The Carolina men's basketball team was coached by the late great Dean Smith. My cousin Billy Highsmith played like Phil Ford, and from 1973 to 1977, Billy played basketball for Guilford College, a small college in Greensboro, North Carolina. He was an amazing basketball player who holds three school records that are still unmatched in the school's basketball program.

When Guilford College was out for the summer, Billy would come home and spend every day, playing with us and teaching us kids in the community the game of basketball. Billy had also gone to college with former NBA champion M. L. Carr who played and eventually coached for the Boston Celtics. M. L. was a key player picked by the Boston Celtics in 1979 during their rebuilding season. The year after M. L. Carr and Larry Bird were picked up by the

Celtics, he led the Celtics to the 1981 Eastern Conference Finals where the Celtics won their fourteenth NBA championship after finishing in the last place in the NBA the previous year. Billy and M. L. became my inspiration for wanting to get better at the game of basketball.

Billy would end up, making future high school stars out of my brother Harvey, my cousin William Newkirk, and me. My cousin William was my idol also. I would eventually follow him into every sport he would play, even baseball. Although for me, basketball was my true love. Growing up in North Carolina at that time was a great place to be if you loved basketball. There were great basketball teachers, motivators, examples, and if we weren't working, that was the opportunity to play ball. We made basketball hoops out of bicycle rims by taking the spokes off the bicycle rim and then nailing it to a tree in our yard. When those rims got old or broken, we had to find another way to play. Some other neighborhood kids had more money than us, so they would have the nicer real basketball rims and nets in their yards and that's where I would spend most of my time. Sometimes we even had the chance to get into the car and drive to other cities around us and compete.

While I adjusted during our first year in North Carolina, making it my priority to give my all to basketball, we occasionally got to see our father. He would come down from New York to see how us kids were doing and also spend time with mom. My parents would go to the local bar, drinking and staying out late and sometimes all night. During one of my father's visits that year, my mother got pregnant with my youngest brother Tavarish. My brother who was now the youngest of eight. Mom left Brooklyn with six kids, and now in total, she had eight kids.

Basketball was the outlet that I needed to escape from the reality that was going on at home. By this time, my father moved permanently to North Carolina from New York, and the violence began. Day in and day out, there was violence between my mother and father. My mother had a part-time job, doing something, and my father found a job, working as a muffler repair man. Their full-time job seemed to be drinking and fighting with each other. My mom

44

spent most of her time at what we call a local bootleggers house, drinking all day until my dad would come home. Immediately, the fighting would start and go on all night. Us kids would run and stay clear of the violence for fear we would get hurt in their crossfire. Hiding got old quickly, and although no one ever wanted to get hurt, there were times as I got older that the fighting would send me to the hospital.

Fall, 1975. By the time seventh grade started at Perderlea Junior High School, my brother Harvey and I had a reputation of being two of the hottest basketball players in and around Wallace, North Carolina. Our junior high school coach, Coach Lunsford, took a strong liking to us. After spending time with Harvey and I and watching us play, he learned about how messed up it was for us at home. It became really easy to see why being on the basketball court became our greatest escape. Coach Lunsford saw that pouring our heart and soul into basketball was the best escape from the craziness and violence at home. Coach could see that we weren't drawn to the streets. Instead, we chose to put our energies into basketball. In turn, coach would let us stay at his house during the week, most likely his attempt to protect us. What coach didn't understand was he was giving us another outlet and more motivation to be even better at basketball. As we continued to play for coach, he exposed us to local colleges and, at one point, even had a local division I coach come and watch us play. A division I college basketball coach, coming to watch some junior high kids play basketball. Yeah, that happened way before LeBron James.

The end of the school year came, and all us kids returned to working in the tobacco fields. The only change was we at least knew what the money we earned would be used for. Our time spent on the tobacco fields that summer would be used for our school clothes and food. It didn't make our time in the tobacco fields any easier. We still felt like slaves, but at least we knew we would have new clothes for the new school year.

CHAPTER 5

S ummer 1977. The summer before eighth grade would be a major turning point for basketball. All the moments in our lives are interconnected in some way. Again, the result of those split-second decisions that have a trickle-down effect on not only our lives but other lives we touch. I just didn't realize at that time that my talent and greatest passion would come back in my life full circle. This summer heading into eighth grade, anytime we had free time from the tobacco fields, Harvey, my cousin William, and me would go to Wilmington, North Carolina to compete against bigger city school kids in basketball tournaments. It was during this summer that I became friends with future NBA players Kenny Gattison, Clyde Simmons, Buzz Peterson, Larry Jordan, and Michael Jordan.

Michael Jordan, who is the image of the NBA and currently part owner of the NBA team the Charlotte Hornets, was just a kid whom I got to compete against. Larry and Michael Jordan's grandmother lived in Wallace, North Carolina and we went to their church, the only church in the area for blacks, with my family. On Sundays, Larry and Michael would come forty-five minutes to go to church with their grandmother so that afterward, they could play ball in the local parks with us. This was our Sunday routine every Sunday during the whole summer.

As my brother and I continued to get better in junior high school, more and more people would start to come watch us play. My brother Harvey was averaging 35 points per game while I was averaging 20 points per game. Spending three years playing for Penderlea Junior High School and being coached by Coach Lunsford was the training ground we needed before entering high school. Over the summer going into high school, we continued our Sunday routine, playing with Michael and Larry after they came from church with their grandma. By this time, Michael stood five feet eleven inches and still seemed to be more focused on baseball rather than basketball. Playing against his brother Larry was Harvey and I. I'm sure he had no choice but to get better and stronger in basketball. The best way to improve your game is to play with guys who can match you and push you to your best. We were all doing that for each other.

My first year in high school was very exciting. Our basketball team spent a lot of time, playing against high schools that had more students than our school. Our high school was a 3A school because of our high student population for the area, but the city schools like New Hanover had more than double our school population and was a 4A school. Kenny Gattison, future NBA player for the Charlotte Hornets, and Clyde Simmons, a future NFL player for the Philadelphia Eagles, both attended New Hanover High School, and both were two sport athletes. Michael and Larry Jordan attended

Laney High School, another 4A school in Wilmington, North Carolina about forty-five miles from my high school.

My brother and I had a great freshman year, playing against these guys, and our summer pickup games got better because of the city guys. My dad had not really paid too much attention to our basketball success because he was busy trying to provide for us and felt like basketball was a waste of time for him to spend watching us. One day, my dad was working at the muffler shop, and a customer came in just to tell my dad about his basketball star sons. The customer went on and on, telling our dad about our basketball skills on the courts. The customer told him about the size of the crowds that came just to see us play. He then asked my dad if he had watched us play, then my dad told him that he had never watched us play. He told my dad that he should take the time to come and see before it was too late. One day, I didn't know how long after he had the conversation with the customers, Harvey and I were out on the playground courts playing. My dad drove up outside the metal fence and watched us play our pickup game. Harvey and I were so excited. This was what we both hoped for, the day our parents would see what we could do, doing something we loved and be proud of us. I think in my dad's own hard way, he was always proud of us. He just wasn't taught to express it, so he didn't say much about it to us, but he did say he liked watching us that day.

Summer, 1978. Going into my final junior high school year, and we all went back to our normal summer routines of cropping tobacco. My brothers and I would spend our time in the fields, talking junk to each other about basketball while we were working. This was our way of escaping our slavery: the manual labor of cropping. After getting done cropping for the day, no matter what time it was, we would compete against other kids in our yard on the dirt court with our makeshift hoop. My dad watched us play one afternoon on the dirt court, and next thing we knew, my dad put up a real basketball hoop in the yard. That was super cool until our dad took it down because we kept arguing and fighting in the front yard.

We got lucky after that because our local church minister put up a nice basketball court at his house. Of course, he had rules too. No cursing, no fighting, and no late nights. Knowing what happened with our dad, we had to follow the minister's rule. It was cool having a hoop so close to home because at times that we couldn't catch a ride into town to play on the concrete courts, we could still play.

My oldest brother Harvey was so much better than me at the game of basketball. His only problem was that he never wanted to put in the work to make himself a better player. I didn't mind putting in the work to make myself the best player, but it was crazy because I always had to put in extra work to keep up with him. Harvey was the first naturally gifted athlete I ever saw. He spent his time, sleeping and chasing girls. But, when he got on the court his talent would take over. Me, on the other hand, could care less about chasing girls. All I wanted to do was play basketball and hope to one day beat him in a one-on-one game.

Summer, 1979. The summer heading into my tenth-grade year in high school, my mom and us kids moved into a place of our own, away from my grandmother. That summer cropping tobacco I spent time, helping my family make money. The local sheriff, June Shaw, was also a black man who had a prosthetic leg. One day on the job, he got his leg shot off and couldn't be a sheriff anymore. Sheriff Shaw was married with a house full of daughters and son. He lived up the street from my grandmother's, and I used to spend a lot of time with his family. Similar to spending time with the Muslim family in the New York brownstone, they took a liking to me. Sheriff Shaw's wife loved me and would cook for me all the time.

Sherriff Shaw had a house in the woods that he would talk about that was ten miles away from my grandmother's house. One day out on his porch, I asked him about the house and what he planned to do with the house since he and his family didn't live there. He was honest and told me he really had no plans for the house. It was just something he owned. I was about fifteen years old at the time and thought it might be an opportunity to get away from my situation. I shared with him that I wanted to find a place for my mother to have her own place. He said, "Let me talk to my wife." He came back to me the next day and tried to slick me. He told me I could crop tobacco for the entire summer for free and then he would let my mother rent the house. His wife overheard our conversation, and she got mad. She wasn't having it and told the sheriff he was not doing that. In front of me, she told him, "You will give him that house, and you will give it to him now! You will also pay him fairly for cropping tobacco all summer long."

The sheriff couldn't argue with her, so I ran back to my mother to let her know that we could move out of my grand-mother's home into our own home immediately. My mother was so proud of me. She was always proud of me, but this meant the world to her. We moved the family away from my grandmother's home immediately.

My dad, who still had a wife and a family, would come around to make sure my mom had money but never moved into the house with us. He was over a lot, but juggling two families didn't allow him to move in. My dad's other family had moved to New York when we moved there and then moved back to North Carolina when my dad moved down permanently. It was just a situation where both his wife and my mom dealt with. It was a time when women stayed with their men, even if they had to share them with another woman. Neither mom nor my dad's wife liked it. But, they knew of each other, and I guess just respected the situation for the sake of keeping my dad in their lives and the lives of his kids.

CHAPTER 6

Summer, 1980. We spent all of our free time this summer at the local courts, catching pickup games every single day of the week. Harvey, William, and I looked for guys, who we could get a great game out of while Michael spent the beginning of his summer, attending the famed Five-Star Camp. This camp was an opportunity to play the best high school basketball players in the country. At the Five-Star Camp, they rotated players in twenty-minute games to give the coaches time to see how the guys played. Michael performed so well, according to the UNC legendary coach Roy Williams that they kept him in the twenty-minute rotations all day. He didn't really see the magic in Michael before the camp, but after that first twenty minutes, Coach Williams was hooked.

It was then that Michael really came into being a star. He had won all the camp awards and one-on-one play awards and was ranked as one of the top ten high school players in the United States. Word soon spread about his celebrity status as a high school baller, but we would continue to get together and play after the camp almost every day. In fact, we played so much even into the night that we petitioned the city council to put up lighting at the park so we could play even later into the night. The city council agreed to put up the lighting, but we had to pay $0.25 cents for half an hour of lights. Everyone who came to play on the courts brought rolls of quarters just to keep the lights on. We played some of the best basketball ever at those parks. I go home today and visit our courts. There are no more lights, and no more pure basketball, getting played on those courts. These days, you only see people, playing soccer.

When I started my junior year in high school, both me and Harvey quit our high school team. Of course, it was hard for me to quit, but without my best friend, my brother Harvey on the team to push me to be my best, I didn't want to play. Our high school coach, Joe Clay Jones, wasn't having it. He didn't care what my reasons were. He was determined to have me back on his team. Coach came to our house every single day to sit and talk with me about getting back on the team. Coach would come around and talk about my options and the places basketball could take me. I ended up getting back on the team without my partner Harvey.

The start of my junior year was very exciting. I was doing well in school and started thinking about actually going to college. I knew the basketball season would be exciting because of all the hype surrounding Michael Jordan. Outside of playing Michael's Laney High School, we also had to square up against Kenny Gattison and his team at New Hanover High. We were scheduled to play both Laney High and New Hanover High twice that season, and boy, was it hyped. A small school, going up against the powerhouse schools all with their own all stars.

We would end up, playing New Hanover first at a local junior high school because our high school chose to build a lunchroom instead of a gym when the school was originally built. New Hanover had some of the biggest high school players I had ever seen. New Hanover's smallest guy was about six feet two inches, and everybody else on the team got bigger from there. Kenny was six feet seven inches, Clyde was six feet five inches, and their other players was as big as well. They had a guard on their team that to this day, Michael Jordan thinks was the best player in the state. This guy should have been in the NBA, but he would later make choices that would keep him from getting there.

New Hanover would end up, beating us both of the times our schools met. Kenny was also in his junior year and being recruited to major colleges, including University of North Carolina and Old Dominion University. He ended up, choosing Old Dominion after his team beat both me and Michael's school to go to the state championships. The most exciting game came when we had to play Laney High. Michael Jordan had been averaging about 28 points per game at the time of our meeting, and he made it look so easy. Every game he played was featured on late-night news, and he was always in the newspaper. Without question, Mike had put his city and high school on the map.

When we got ready to play them, we had to use another high school's gym again. Even though the game was scheduled for a larger gym, it was packed beyond capacity all the way out the doors the day of our game. At the beginning of the game, Michael met us at the circle and said, "I'm gonna get my thirty points and call it a night." We all laughed because at that time, he was averaging 28.9 points a game. He got 28 in the third quarter of the game, so his coach sat him down. It was an amazing game, looking back on it today. I remember one play that still sticks in my mind even today. One of his teammates had shot a jumper, and it bounced off the back of the rim, but before anybody could get into position to get the rebound, you saw these to long arms come out of nowhere went above the rim and slammed the ball back in the rim. Michael had a forty-two-inch vertical at that time and could get up quickly. They won the game handedly. One of the players on Michael's team, Leroy Smith, was the player who kept Michael off the team when he tried out as a sophomore. Leroy was six feet four inches as a sophomore while Michael was only five feet eleven inches. He went on to play college at the University of Charlotte. Man, that was an amazing game.

We finished our junior year season great. We went to the high school playoffs, and I was all conference. We continued to follow my friends Kenny Gattison and Michael Jordan because they would play each other to see who would go to state for the 4A division. It was funny because when Michael Jordan played Kenny Gattison's team, those guys physically beat him to the point where he would only get maybe twenty points against them. New Hanover was filled with a lot of football players who made Mike play a very physical game. New Hanover would later go on to beat Laney High and play for the 4A state title. Unfortunately, New Hanover ended up losing the North Carolina state title to the Jacksonville, North Carolina, high school basketball team. New Hanover High also lost to them in the state title game for football.

Summer, 1981. The summer before my senior year. Again, I would spend a lot of time on the basketball courts. Kenny Gattison was meeting up with us at the courts because like me, he was going into his senior year. Michael didn't come by that often because he started his freshman year at the University of North Carolina. Michael's brother Larry, however, came around all the time because he was like me, a basketball junkie, and we would have some great fun on and off the court. On Wednesday nights, we would take our game indoors to a local gym called Rose Hill Magnolia. Man, talk about seeing all of the up-and-coming high school basketball stars. If you thought you could play here, you would find out quickly. We would see all the best local high school ballers, some old former college greats, and then throw in Larry Jordan with his forty-five-inch vertical, and boy, was it good. We would go for hours like we were getting paid, and the smack talking was the best. If a player knew he could get you out of your game psychologically, you were done, and if you lost, the guys, waiting to get on would never pick you up. You generally went to the gym with a couple of your own guys, hoped the team you picked was good, and maybe get in one or two games. If you were that lucky, that would be it for you because the winning team would stay on till they were beaten, and even they may not be able to get back on the court again. Rose Hill Magnolia gym was legendary in southeastern North Carolina.

With my senior year approaching, I began thinking about what it was I wanted to do with my life. My dream was the same as Michael Jordan and Kenny Gattison—go to college so that one day I could help my family. It was my dream, and I had the passion, but I just wasn't sure if I could succeed. I remember discussing it with my coach, and he was sure I could do it, so I leaned on his belief as my own. I started working on it, figuring out what's next for me, what college I would go to, and live my dreams. When the season started, I focused on the fun of playing. We played all of the big schools again, and it was always cool, playing against Kenny and Clyde. Those guys were so tough. They were already pretty much recruited to the schools they wanted, and they never took their foot off the gas. We played them early in my senior season, and once again, they defeated us. I had an awesome game, but it wasn't enough to beat them. Today, Kenny Gattison jokes about our team. He says we had two-and-a-half players on our team: me and my brother Harvey and the coach's son. We finished our season, fighting our way to the district semifinals. My last high school game, we played James Kenan High School for the second to last round in the district championship. The game was tough. We were on the same level with wins and losses in the season. In the end, James Kenan High School basketball team beat us in the semifinals, then they lost in the finals.

With my high school basketball career coming to an end, and graduation quickly approaching, I continued to play basketball in the local parks, not knowing what to do about going to college. Even though the regular basketball season was over, I continued to play when I got chosen as a player in multiple high school all-star games. These games were opportunities for college basketball scouts to see some of the best talent to fill up their roster for the next year. I received multiple offers from colleges, and I got to go to three of the colleges to play in front of the entire college recruiting staff and coaches. Those three schools offered me full scholarships to play ball for their schools.

Just before we went on the school visit to Chowan College, my dad had put me in the situation of you either do this, or something else. You either go to school or go to work. I didn't like it because it wasn't my choice. He wasn't supporting me. He just wanted to control me and my decisions for my life.

When Chowan offered me a full ride to play ball for their school, my dad asked me, "You aren't going to take the scholarship?"

I said, "No, I don't want to play basketball."

So he said, "You are going to do something."

We rode back from Virginia, five hours, and he just yelled at me the entire ride. I told my mother I was just tired of it.

After graduation, instead of taking the scholarship, I took off and went to New York. I started playing in New York. I got really good up there while I was living with my aunt Thelma. Neighbors started seeing me play at night, and I started drawing a crowd to watch me play. My aunt Doris asked why everybody was going to the court late at night. Someone told her, "They're going to see your nephew play." I remember Eddie Murphy and Saturday Night Live was the hottest thing on television at 11:00 p.m. At that time, instead of people in the neighborhood, watching Eddie Murphy, they were in the park next to my aunt's house, watching me play.

While playing near my aunt's house, I met a guy they called Bear. I never got his real name. He had been a star at Long Island University where it was said he averaged 28 points per game until his knee gave out. He used to come by at night and participate in some of the games he saw me play. He eventually asked me if I would be willing to play in the Rucker League in uptown New York. I knew what the Rucker was, and I didn't hesitate to agree to play on his team. The Rucker is legendary for having the best basketball players from New York come out and play in summer league games. Out of the Rucker have been some basketball legends: Dr. J, Lloyd

World B. Free, Kenny Anderson, Kenny Smith, Dwayne "The Pearl" Washington, and a host of other stars. To get into the league, you had to have exceptional talent, so to be asked was an honor. So I spent the summer of 1982, playing at the Rucker. It felt like being back in high school, playing with major talents like Jordan and Gattison. I developed a following at the Rucker, and then one of those split-second decisions changed everything for me.

I hooked up with my cousin who had spent his whole life being on the other side of the law. Bobby said he had a sweet deal where we could make a lot of money. The deal was there was a sneaker factory up the street, and all we needed to do was climb in and take some of the sneakers. I could throw them out to him from the back window, and he had a guy he could sell them to. Once he sold the sneakers, we could split the money. I climbed into the window and threw the sneakers out to my cousin who put them in the boxes. We did all that and didn't get caught. We left with the sneakers and went to my cousin's girlfriend house. He had me wait there until he sold the sneakers.

One bad thing I didn't consider: my cousin was a crackhead. He sold the sneakers but never came back with the cash. He took off with the money and smoked it up while leaving me at his girl's house. When I finally caught up to Bobby, I beat the bricks off him. I beat him so bad, he ended up in the hospital, and my aunt put me out her house. He knew why because by the time I saw him, he didn't have no money. I ended up, staying at my other aunt's house who lived close by. And when I came outside my aunt's house the next day, I saw my parents, sitting in the car, waiting for me. My cousin's mom called them down south, told them what had happened, and my parents drove all night to come get me.

My dad was so pissed, he wouldn't even let me explain. Every time I tried to explain, all I got was a slap in my mouth. My mom was more levelheaded. She ended up getting pissed at my aunt, her sister. Mom said my cousin must have done something to me for me to behave like that, but my dad wasn't hearing it. For the whole ten-hour drive he cursed, yelled, and hit me. Of course, since nobody else knew what was going on, I just looked like I was starting some trouble up in NYC. The closer we came to North Carolina, all I felt was that I was stuck.

Once back in North Carolina, I had no job or idea what I was going to do with myself, but one thing I did know and that was I was going to get away from my dad and that small town, and I didn't care how I was going to do it. In the meantime, I went back to what I knew—back to the basketball court. Most of the time, I was out, shooting hoops all by myself. I needed the time alone with just me and the ball. It was my only escape.

One of those days, playing alone, one of my friends approached me and asked, "Why don't you go to college and play basketball?"

I told him the same thing I had told my dad, "I don't want to go to college. I just wanted to find a way to make money and help out my mom."

This dude came back at me with, "You know, you can make money and play basketball in the Navy!"

I didn't know that, but it was all I needed to hear. This was perfect. I could make money and help out my mom, and since I was pissed at my dad, it was the motivation I needed to sneak off, take the test, and sign up to join the Navy. I scored so high on the entrance test that they told me I could pick any job that I wanted. I knew I didn't like getting dirty, and I was really good at math, so one recruiter suggested I become a quartermaster. A quartermaster is the guy who drives the Navy ships and aircraft carriers. They are skilled in navigation and must use their math skills to calculate speed, time, and distance for the ship to arrive at its appointed location on time. I loved the ideal of being a quartermaster, so I listed it as my job choice.

September 23, 1983. I asked my dad to take me to the bus station the next morning so I could leave North Carolina. Naturally, my dad asked me where I was going. For the first time since I went to inquire about the Navy, I finally told my mom and dad that I had enlisted in the US Navy. I didn't need their permission, since I was nineteen years old at that time. My dad was shocked and very hurt. Why wouldn't I have trusted him sooner with that information? My mother, although I am sure she was sad to see me go, was also very happy for me. She knew I wasn't going to stay in Wallace and get lost.

While my brother Harvey was so upset with me that he didn't talk to me for several years, even when I came home for leave. If he was at home, he would get up and leave whatever room I was in. My brother Harvey had been my live-in best friend. We did everything together. As long as I was in the house, I was his rock to get through the violence at home. With me out of the house, it would be his job to handle the violence between our parents. Harvey felt I abandoned him when I left.

My dad eventually agreed to take me to the bus station. He along with my mom, brothers, and sisters all came to the Bus station to see me off. When I got on that bus to leave, I finally felt free, and I knew it would be a long time before I would return home. It was my time to decide who I was going to be. Prayerfully, it still included basketball.

CHAPTER 7

Making the decision to go into the Navy was pretty easy for me. It was one of those decisions fueled by anger, compassion, passion, and empowerment. I was angry at my dad for trying to control my life without giving me an option for my future. I felt compassion for my mom and felt like this was my opportunity to make her proud and support her needs. I felt my passions for basketball being fueled again. This was my opportunity to kill two birds with one stone: help my mom and play ball. I felt empowered because although I didn't know where this decision would lead me, I knew I had the power to make it. A split-second decision that would have a trickle-down effect on everyone that loved me.

I was not only leaving my dad, who had pissed me off, I was leaving my mom, brothers, and sisters. I left my best friend Jeff Newton and his cousin Janaria, my high school sweetheart. When I made my silent decision to join the Navy, I didn't give a second thought to all of those who would be hurt. Janaria and I started dating in my junior year in high school even though we met through Jeff in junior high school. Jeff Newton and his brothers were the biggest group of people most of us in junior high had ever seen. He was one of a lot of kids in his family because his dad had lots of kids like my dad. Everyone was afraid to fight anyone in Jeff's family. That was until he and I met. He pissed me off somehow, and I stood up to him and said I'm gonna beat the bricks off you at break. Jeff was cool with it and came out to meet me along with absolutely everyone in the school. All the kids heard about my need to commit suicide and fight this little giant.

It was like one of those old school flicks, where it felt like we were moving in slow motion toward each other, the wind was coming out from nowhere, and the tension was growing the closer we got to each other. I had heart, and he had size, so this battle would be epic. Right up until Ms. Brooks, our science teacher, came out and pulled both of us over to the water fountain. Ms. Brooks was no small woman. She played tennis in her spare time and was notoriously heavy-handed. When she paddled you, it was like she was working out her backhand swing and would lift you off the ground with each hit. She told us we would get paddled right out there in front of the whole school. You know that moment right before an event where you look at the person next to you and it's the quietest moment and you take a breath just before all hell breaks loose? I looked at Jeff, and he looked at me, and next, it was all burn and pain. From that point forward, we were best friends. We experienced a moment together that no one else on the planet would understand, so we had no choice but to be best friends. After that, Jeff introduced me to Janaria, his cousin, whom I would end up dating in my junior and senior year in high school.

Janaria was tall and beautiful, and we were great friends going back to Penderlea Junior High. Being friends since junior high school and then dating in high school meant we really loved and respected each other. I wanted to tell her I was leaving for the Navy, but I was afraid to tell her because I was afraid she was going to break up with me, and I would lose our lifetime friendship. I finally made the decision to tell her. My mother told me I needed to tell her. I went over to her house to tell her, sat on the couch, and told her. She started crying. She didn't know what she was going to do after graduation, and she was stuck there with her mom. She was at home and comfortable. I always wanted more, even though I didn't know what more was. I don't think she wanted more. I knew she wanted to get out of her mom's house and get her own place, but I don't think she really had the ambition to make change. If I had let her, she would have stayed with me and been content. Her focus would have been that she would make a good wife, like her mom did for her dad.

As the time got closer, she resolved to understand that I needed to find more. I told her we should break up, but she said no. She said she would be fine there until I came back home. So we remained a couple even after I left for boot camp, heading to Orlando, Florida. It hurt like hell, and I missed her so much, but like she said, I was bound to do something with my life that would take me away from her. I just needed to take care of my business and then come back to her.

Boot camp in the eighties was pure hell! That is not an exaggeration. That is pure truth. It was sixteen weeks of retraining your mind away from being a civilian to be a military soldier who could use their skills and training in a moment's notice wherever the military needed you. The training was amazing, and if you have ever been in the military, even if it was only for a short time, you have that skill for a lifetime. For the first eight weeks of the training, you were not allowed to communicate with anyone outside of your command. I suppose it would disrupt the training process. After eight weeks, you were required to connect with your loved ones and tell them you were alive.

I boarded the bus to boot camp on September 23, 1983, and the two days I spent on the bus was like reliving my entire life in my head. The experiences both good and bad flashed through my head and stopped when we arrived in Orlando, Florida, and our process into the United States military began promptly at 5:59 a.m. The training officers boarded the bus, and the yelling and cursing began. We got off the bus in a single file line, and I swear from the very first moment of the sixteen weeks until the last, I was tested. My testing was different than everyone else's. My test was to see if all of the harsh experiences I had at home were preparation for what the military was going to throw at me. There were 150 males in my training group, and every day that we learned to eat, shower, and shave in three minutes, it seemed that we lost another person. Every time we were subjected to physical punishment because one guy couldn't complete his tasks timely, we lost another guy. For me, I passed the test. I could take the yelling, the cursing, the physical punishments, and the endurance training because I dealt with versions of this all my life.

There was one test they seem to find that made me question myself and whether or not this was something I could do. Me, the guy who seemed to push his way into every opportunity available to play basketball. Me, the guy who could stand up to our tough-as-nails dad and gain his respect. The test was to see if I could swim or float. I knew I couldn't do either. In all my life, I never learned to swim. I remember it was my turn to walk up the ladder to the platform where we would need to jump into a pool that had to be no less than twenty feet deep. I climbed the ladder, got to the edge of the platform, and looked down into the crystal-clear pool. I could see that underneath the water, there were guys in scuba gear. I'm sure they would catch those who couldn't swim like me and bring them to the surface just before we drowned. I heard my commanding officer yell for me to step off the platform, but I refused. I didn't move from the platform. I just didn't jump. I really wasn't refusing to jump. I was refusing to drown.

Apparently, I was pissing off my commanding officer because after seeing I was refusing to jump off the platform, my commanding officer stepped onto the first step of the ladder. This is when you realize who and what you are really afraid of. I shouldn't have been afraid of anyone after dealing with my dad. That time, he figured out I was skipping school in New York and told me he would kill me should have been the most terrifying moment in my life. I could not imagine any time in my life being scarier than that moment until this one. I figured out in that moment, standing on the platform one step away from drowning that my commanding officer was who I was truly afraid of. Each step he took up the ladder to the platform increased my terror until I figured out I was more afraid of him than I was of drowning. I took that step off the platform and plunged into the pool. I didn't feel the temperature of the water. The only thought I had was how deep I went with each passing second. I am sure I was only sinking for a second or two, but it felt like an eternity to me. The guys in the scuba gear grabbed me and pulled me over to the side of the pool. I failed the swim-and-float test.

I got out of the pool and then learned that was only half of the test. My commanding officer, who I assumed was still pissed at me, told me that I had three days to learn how to float for two minutes. Every day I didn't pass the two-minute test would mean extra work for everyone else in my group. If I didn't pass the test within the three days, I would be discharged from boot camp and sent home. I was ashamed because I was making my guys suffer because of me. As if boot camp wasn't hard enough now, they were going to put more on everyone just because in nineteen years, I never learned how to swim and float. On top of that embarrassment, the fear of going home empty handed was too much. I would let my mom and family down. I would never be able to play ball. My life might as well be over.

For the next three days, I had to get up at 4:00 a.m. to learn how to float in a pool of water for two minutes—120 seconds. Something that seemed so simple and short was the concrete wall, keeping me from everything else I wanted for my life. The first and second day I went to the pool, I couldn't do it. I got four attempts each day, and I failed all four times. I had to walk back and look at the guys who were suffering with extra work all because I couldn't float in a pool of water for two minutes. The third day, I didn't know if it was because I just couldn't stand, looking those guys in the eyes and seeing their disappointment in me one more day. It could have been the sheer terror of thinking that after this day, I would be sent home if I couldn't float for two minutes, but on the last of four attempts on the last day, I conquered it. I passed the test, which meant I got to stay.

When I came back and faced the guys after passing the test, my relief could be felt in the air. Everyone was so excited and happy for me. They weren't angry for having suffered additional physical punishments because of me. They were purely happy for me and my accomplishment. When my commanding officer found out I passed the test, he made it a point to let all of us know how proud he was. He was proud of our group for pulling together to support me as I passed the test. He was also proud because as a result of experiencing this test together, our group was made stronger as a unit.

Finally, after sixteen weeks, it is was time for the bittersweet day of graduation. Graduation from boot camp is a major ordeal. You get to invite your family and friends to celebrate your achievement. You did it! You made it through sixteen weeks of hell, and on the other side, your mind is ready to take on whatever the military throws at you to give you the opportunity to support your family and make them proud. The only challenge for me: there was nobody there to celebrate my accomplishment. It was my fault because when I had the chance to communicate with my family, the only person I wrote a letter to was my mom just to let her know I was doing okay. There was no one there for me to celebrate and see for the last time as I knew the next step was for me to travel to my active duty station further away than I had ever traveled in my life. I was going to San Diego, California, thousands of miles away from home. I would truly be on my own. There was no family, friends, or loves of my life. It was exciting and scary at the same time. It was time to move forward in my life.

When I arrived in San Diego, there was no time for rest. I learned we were leaving for a six-month deployment. We would spend six months at sea, stopping at different ports around the world and supporting the Marines in their campaigns. I reported to my first boss and now lifelong friend Petty Officer James Patrick Bohanan. It was his job to train me to be a great quartermaster and to conform to the Navy's code of conduct on the ship. Bohanan was responsible for ten sailors, including me, and he made that six months float by. Our first stop was the beautiful island of Hawaii. I worked in my quartermaster position for two weeks, getting from San Diego to Hawaii. When we docked, my job was done until it was time to travel to the next port, so I took advantage.

CHAPTER 8

It's amazing how your passions drive your life. How no matter what decisions you make, your passions are still ever present. Once we got underway for my first six-month tour, Bohannon and I spent a lot of time together. I was learning my job, and we were talking about basketball. One day, we were talking about it, and he made the suggestion that we should get a ship's team together. I loved the idea and asked what that would take. He went to our chief to discuss the idea. The chief didn't like sports, but he liked Bohannan, so he gave him the go-ahead. Next, he needed the captain's buy-in. The ship's captain agreed on one condition: Bohannon would need to be the ship's athletic director. That would mean that any sport that happened on the ship would have to come through him. It also meant that Bohannon could order whatever equipment and supplies we needed to get the best for our sports teams.

We started recruiting players for our new basketball team. We started going to all of the different departments, finding out who played ball. By the time we had tryouts, there was all manner of talent on the ship. We even had a guy who played pro ball for a year from Detroit. Tryouts took place on board the ship's hanger deck. The hanger deck was a huge place in the middle of the ship that all of the aircrafts that weren't ready to be flown were stored. We rolled two basketball rims out and measured the right distance for the hoops to be in regulation distance. We had fifty guys, including myself, trying out for the team. Man, I felt like I was right back, competing with Jordan, Gattison, or the talent at the Rucker. It was tough, competing with guys who had been playing for college, and others who had already went pro. The tryouts took two days, and I made it on the team. Bohannon, being from Atlanta, since he was the guy who put the team together, said he wanted to pick the uniforms. He was an Atlanta Hawks fan, so he picked the bright-orange, red, and black colors of the Atlanta Hawks. We all agreed we would be the Atlanta Hawks.

The coach of the team was going to also be a player as well. His name was Mark Hopkins. Mark was six feet four inches, lean, and very athletic. He was from Philadelphia and had played some college ball himself. Mark also got selected to play for the Navy in what was called the All-Navy team. This team consisted of the navy's finest basketball players. The All-Navy team included players stationed on both land and ships. Once a year, the Navy would invite the best basketball players in the service to try out for this All-Navy team; however, only twelve players per season would be picked to represent the Navy. These guys would travel all over the world and even play against the US Olympic basketball team if there was going to be an Olympics that year. The All-Navy team would also play against other inter-military branches like the Army, Marines, Air Force, and even the Coast Guards teams. When you are selected to play for the All-Navy team, if you are on a ship, and your ship goes out to sea, they will have you airlifted from the ship when it's time for the tryouts and fly you there. It doesn't matter where you are in the world. They will fly you to the place where tryouts are being held as long as the ship's captain authorized your travel. I got the honor one year to play for the All-Navy team.

Now it doesn't matter if you're playing at the Rucker, the NBA, college, high school, or in the military, basketball is about heart, talent, and much trash talking. Trash talking comes from the players and also the fans. For us, it was the ship's captain, and he hadn't even seen us play. Our captain would call other ship's captain and warn them to get their teams ready because when we see them in port, it's on! He would brag that he had a really great team. Again, not having seen us play. That's some serious trash talking. We just had to get our team together to make sure we could always back him up.

We would get into a port, rent out a space, and one of the ships hosts a tournament. Our captain was so confident he had the best team that he would bet the other captains that we would win. After he made a bet, he would come to me and say, "Marvin I hope you are really good." That was code for, "You better win. I just bet on you." We backed it up. The first season against the other ships, our record was 86–2.

In 1985, my second year in the Navy, my ship was set to dock in Bremerton, Washington. All I heard was Washington, and since I never heard of Bremerton, Washington, I thought we were going to Washington, D.C. Going to D.C. would put me closer to my family, and I could reconnect with everyone after just two years. To my surprise, Bremerton was in Washington State, the Pacific Northwest. Likely the farthest place in the United States from my family back in Wallace, North Carolina. Our ship was long overdue for repairs, and naval shipyard in Bremerton was the best place on the West Coast to get everything done. Our captain gave all of the ship's personnel a housing allowance so that we could choose how we wanted to live during our more than a year's stay in Bremerton. I made the choice to get an apartment and live off the ship during my time.

Being stationed in Bremerton didn't stop our team from competing with local community colleges and church basketball teams. The naval shipyard had an amazing gym, and at one point, we even hosted our own basketball tournament at the naval shipyard.

In Bremerton, the position of naval shipyard was downtown. There were major shopping stores that line the streets outside the gates of the shipyard and a ferry post that allowed citizens to ride across the Puget Sound from Bremerton to downtown Seattle. My buddies and I were riding up the street to the ferry one afternoon when I saw her. She was walking down the sidewalk, heading into Bremerton, and I had Bohannon stop the car he was driving us around in. It took him some time to stop the car, but I jumped out and ran up the hill to talk to her. The minute I saw her, I knew I was in love. This was the first time in my life I had ever experienced love at first site. I mean I loved Janaria, but this was completely different. When I caught up to her, it was a blessing from God because after talking for a minute, she gave me her phone number.

68

Now I was in love, but I had a problem—I was engaged at that time. My second year in the military, I was talking to my dad on the phone about Janaria. Dad told me Janaria was a good girl, and I needed to make things right with her. Either marry her or go on with my life. I knew he was right because she had put her life on hold for me. So, I called her and asked her to marry me. We had decided that the following year we would get married. I was all in and committed until I saw her.

Her name was Andrea, and I liked everything about her. She was still in high school, but she was perfect for me. I started spending more and more time with her and hanging out with her friends. I was just in love, and I didn't care about anything else. I fell so madly and deeply in love that I forgot I was engaged. I forgot until one day, my love haze came down, and I woke up to the most intense guilt. I had to tell her I wasn't completely free to be in this relationship, at least not until I told her all of the truth. I finally told Andrea, and she was so hurt. She ran to her mother and told her that I was engaged to another girl.

You know how you play it in your mind, telling someone the truth. You try to tell them in a way that will hurt the least, they either cry or yell, then after, you tell them how you are going to fix it. Yeah, that conversation didn't go at all the way I had planned. Instead of dealing with the situation with Andrea, I had her mother come at me mad as a hornet. She was pissed that I was messing with her daughter while I was engaged to someone else. The only way out was to promise both of them I would fix it right away. I was afraid that I might lose both of them in this situation.

I felt like the lowest and most terrible person in the world. In my heart, I knew it was the right thing to do. Janaria was crying on the phone because we were so close to our wedding day. The only thing we had left to do was for me to come home, get my suit, and go to the preacher. That was how close we were to getting married. I told her I could lie to her and be up here doing things and cheating on her but that wouldn't be right. I told her, "You may not appreciate me now, but someday, you will get over this and figure out I did the right thing." My family was so mad at me. My mom stopped calling me for three to four months, and my dad cut off all communication for about a year.

When I went back to Ms. Phillips, Andrea's mother's house, I begged for her forgiveness and told her that I broke off the engagement. I truly loved Andrea with all my heart, and I would have done just about anything to get back in her good graces. Ms. Philips wasn't happy with me, but she was such a wonderful woman and mom, and she gave me a second chance to win Andrea's heart back. I could tell Andrea was still mad and hurt, but she did give me another chance to love her.

It was just about time for our ship to leave Bremerton, and Andrea told me she was pregnant. I was excited because I was having a child with the absolute love of my life, but my job was getting in my way. The ship was being reassigned to San Diego, California, and I had to do something to stay connected and help her. Just before I was leaving for a deployment that would end up back in San Diego, California, I asked Andrea to marry me. If she married me, then she and my son would be covered under my medical benefits, and they would get the best possible medical care.

We got married in a small ceremony because I couldn't afford anything big, and I knew my family couldn't afford to come. I wore a suit, and she had a dress that showcased her growing belly. It was perfect for me simply because she was everything I needed—the love of my life. I left on my deployment and got a telegraph stating that on Father's Day, June 19, 1986, she gave birth to my son, Marvin Gaye Williams Jr. This was the proudest day of my entire life.

My third year in the Navy, my chief started approaching me, saying maybe I shouldn't be in the Navy. He told me he thought I would be better suited for playing basketball in college. By this time, we had pulled back into the San Diego port and some college basketball team wanted us to be the host for one of their tournaments. This tournament included the University of Mississippi (Old Miss), Arizona State University, San Diego State University, and the University of Michigan. These were national college basketball powerhouses, and they invited our ship's team to come and compete in the tournament. Our team rose to challenge and played our hearts out. We played so well, all of the college's scouts came to the ship. The colleges were so interested in me that they asked my chief if there was any way that I could get out of my Navy contract. My captain called Washington, D.C. to see what the options were for me. My captain cashed in some favors, and in the end, they let me out of my contract.

I got an invitation from Arizona State University and a preliminary full-ride scholarship offer to play basketball. I went on a school visit and got to spend time with the coach. I told the coach that I have a family and would only be able to take his offer if my family, my wife and son, could come live on the campus with me. The coach didn't hesitate. He said he would make accommodations for my family because he really wanted me to play for the school. It was perfect because now, Andrea and I could make a home with each other, and I could spend more time with my son.

I picked Arizona State. They had a guard that I really liked. I got to play against him. He played like Michael Jordan's brother Larry. So me and him became really cool. He was telling me how wonderful Arizona was and then the coach, Steve Patterson, was great too. A big six-foot-nine-inch dude just as sweet as he could be. I called them up and told them I accepted their offer, and everyone was excited. After that, I talked with Andrea about the offer. I told her they had a family apartment ready for us when got there. It would be more than enough space to accommodate me, her, and little Marvin. Her response shocked me. She told me I could go myself. She and my son weren't going to leave Bremerton, her mother, and everything she knew. She had everything she needed right there, and she didn't want to leave. Her and her mother always supported any dream I had, and I loved that. So she wanted me to go and live my dream.

I loved my family and I loved her, and I didn't want to leave them. I figured I could find another place to play basketball because all I wanted was to be with my family. I called Coach Patterson and apologized to him because I couldn't accept the offer. When I came back to Bremerton, Andrea and her mom had already worked it out. I could get on the basketball team at Olympic College (OC). Olympic College (OC) was a local college in Bremerton that would play other college teams around the state of Washington. Andrea's twin brother, Andre, was playing basketball at a college in Tacoma, a city about thirty minutes outside of Bremerton. If I was at OC, he and I would be able to compete with each other. I reached out to OC basketball coach and did what I needed to do to get on the OC basketball team.

I think Andrea felt bad that she didn't want to go with me to Arizona to play, so she really supported me, playing at OC. She had told me I could go to Arizona, and they would take care of little Marvin. She didn't want me to be disappointed. What she didn't understand was it didn't matter where I was playing, as long as I had them, I had no choice but to be successful. It was like the story in the book *Think and Grow Rich* by Napoleon Hill. If you have burned the bridges behind, then you have no choice but to move forward and be successful. And that is what I did. I had to move forward and be successful. As long as I had my family, I knew I could be.

CHAPTER 9

When you grow up in an environment that is hard, that is abusive, where you see your parents always struggling for money, and where the people you look up to and trust the most don't know how to love each other, it affects you. Their actions affect you in ways that you can't describe. We all have that story, that sequence of events that subconsciously controls how you see yourself, your surroundings, and other people. The effects of the split-second decisions made by persons before us. Playing basketball always seemed to balance my surroundings. It always gave me a way to put my environment, my family, and myself in check, at least long enough for me to feel like I was in balance. How do you keep your balance when the new circumstance you got to deal with, a wife and son, is something you never seen done well? How do you keep in balance when the most important thing you need to do is to take care of them in a way you have never experienced before? How do you keep all of the negative stuff you experienced away from this new and wonderful life? You don't. You can't. Because in truth, you're not mature enough to know that all the shit you went through is all over you like a cloak. If you don't even know it's there, how can you fix it so it doesn't now ruin your amazing family?

Well, if someone figures that out, will you let me know? Because the truth is I'm still trying to figure it out. Back when my son was born, I didn't have a clue that I was like my dad and didn't trust telling most people what I was going through. I didn't have a clue about how to have a happy family. I never saw one. No man in my family was touchy-feely, or a big hugger. How are you going to do something for someone else you ain't never seen? The only thing I saw that was good for a man to do as a husband and a father. I knew my job was to be a provider.

Damn, it seemed like right from the beginning, Andrea and I was struggling. I was trying to learn how to be a good husband on the fly. Again, how are you going to be a good husband when you never seen a good husband? My father had nineteen kids and maintained two families. He was married to a woman who wasn't happy about his relationship with my mom but stayed with him and accepted all is faults. My dad was with my mom, and they were alcoholics and physically abusive to each other. My grandfather was the boss, and my grandmother did whatever he said to do. That was how it was: women just did what the man said. I didn't have, nor did I really want a woman who was just a servant to me. I didn't want a woman who put aside all of her needs, thoughts, gifts, and family just so she could be with me. I didn't want a woman who I could curse at, lay all my issues and burdens on, and fight with just to say we have been together forever. I didn't want that, but I wasn't mature enough to say what I did want, or how to have the happy family life I thought of in my head.

The only thing I seemed to be able to control at that time was that I could still play basketball. I loved my wife, and I loved my son. I would go home every day to try to show them I loved them with all of my heart, but I would walk through the door, and it would just be a fight. Andrea describes it now:

"He was just angry and demanding all of the time. He was always so negative. I wasn't always positive because I also had a lot going on. I didn't have my high school diploma because I dropped out when I had little Marvin. We had to live on and off with my mother, but no matter what, I was going to take care of my son even on those days when I didn't have the money to buy Pampers. But when Marvin came home, he was always angry about something. He was always mad at me. There just wasn't a time at home when he was just happy, or so it seemed. I never questioned if he loved us. I just couldn't figure out why the hell he was so mad all of the time. I loved him, but I knew I couldn't stay struggling and mad all of the time. The only time we didn't fight was when that dude was playing basketball."

74

I remember one day she and I were fighting at her mother's house, and she was holding my son. In the middle of the fight, I remembered being caught in the middle when my parents were arguing. I remember what it felt like watching them. I remember thinking, *I didn't want that for my son when the only picture he remembered of both of us were the times when we were fighting.* In my head, I said, *I have to make a change.* I remember thinking, *Neither of them deserves this.* They deserve a better me. They deserve a lover in me that makes life better, not worse for them. They didn't deserve someone who was going to mess up their lives.

Now, thinking back on that time, I remember thinking all of those things, but actual change requires maturity, and I didn't have it. I was mature enough to handle, seeing someone get blasted in a fight. I was mature enough to handle, seeing the abuse between my parents. I was mature enough to leap off of the platform into a pool when I knew I couldn't swim. But being mature enough to admit to the person you love that you got a problem you don't know how to fix, going to get professional help in order to make your relationship stronger, and figuring out how to stop using your passion as an escape hatch to get away from all your problems and forgetting they exist if only for a moment. Nope, not me. Instead, I just kept repeating the cycle of abuse that I saw.

My first year playing basketball at OC, I got really close with my coach, Dave Sturgeon. Dave was in his forties and very health conscious. He and I clicked immediately. I had a full scholarship to play basketball, and it felt like I was on the right track to my dreams. My mother-in-law, who was one of the most amazing persons I have ever met, was my angel. Whenever I needed to talk, or get a fresh perspective on an issue, Ms. Phillips was my go-to. She reminded me of Ms. Chiney, our local preacher in Wallace, North Carolina. When Ms. Phillips said jump, you jumped. She was also super kind and caring as she would share the right word of God at the perfect time. She was forgiving, loving, stern, and patient. I know God blessed me with her. She also loved the game of basketball. She was always in the stands, cheering me and her son, Andre, on. I am sure it was difficult to decide who to cheer for when we were playing each other, but it worked. Ms. Philips was the first person I talked to after I got accepted at OC.

Our first basketball season ended 3–21. There were numerous reasons why we had a poor year. Coach Sturgeon was hired late in the season. I came on just before the season started. My teammate Eric Cole was an amazing five-foot-nine-inch gritty point guard with a beautiful jump shot. We didn't get a chance to connect with our teammates. There were simply lots of reasons, but what we lacked in wins, we gained in a solid team. We all really embraced our coach and genuinely loved playing ball with each other. I was the only player who was married with a family, and after the disappointment of the season, that was about to change.

By the end of my first year in school, Andrea and I decided to get a divorce. When it was all said and done, I knew us getting a divorce was all my fault. I knew it had nothing to do with her. It all had to do with me. I was the issue. She gave me everything I could have asked for. I just didn't know how to handle or manage it. The one good thing was even though Andrea and I weren't going to be married, I never lost her support, or the support of her family. Ms. Philips still treated me like her son, and Andrea's brothers and sister never stopped talking to me. They still included me in their lives especially Andre, who I was still competing with on the basketball court since he received a scholarship at Peirce Community College in Tacoma, Washington. With this major change in my situation, the most important thing was that I still had full access to my son. Andrea even set it up so that I would have my son with me six months of the year so that it wouldn't put too much pressure on me while I was attending school.

With the change in my situation, Coach Sturgeon stepped in and helped both Andrea and me financially with my son's needs. The OC athletic directors gave me a job. I got lucky because even though it was one of the toughest times in my life, God seen fit to surround me with angels. I knew it wasn't going to be easy, but I had the support I needed to keep loving and taking care of my son. I could support Andrea, who was still the love of my life, the best way I knew how. I also had a family unit that I could lean on, and I still had basketball. I also gained some unexpected support from my Navy buddies when they learned where I had landed, playing ball. My buddies Lee Glossett, Mark Hopkins, and Mason Brown were guys I played with in the Navy. They came and watched me play, which meant the world to me.

I made the transition from being married to single again and got my grind on in the gym. With the season over, I never stopped making sure I was ready for anything basketball had to throw at me. One day, Andre brought a girl around that went to his school. Valarie was a beautiful girl. She was mixed with both Mexican and African-American heritages. She was an athlete who played two sports at Olympic College. Valarie and I started dating, and I was completely upfront with her. I told her I had a son and my ex-wife lived in Bremerton. I let her know that although we were no longer married, we were still connected, and she and her family were still my family. Andre had already told her the situation with his sister, but I wanted her to know from me. There was no time to make the mistake of thinking Andrea was not still a huge part of my life and my support system along with being the mother of my son. Valarie had been adopted as a child and was very open to the blended family idea. She was amazing with my son, and I was grateful for her being in my life.

My second season with OC was in 1989. This year would be the most excited and final season with OC. Coach Sturgeon spent his summer, recruiting the most talented players he could find. He got this kid from Seattle Prep High School: six-foot-seven-inch Dan Jones. Dan had a seven-inch wingspan, was super aggressive, and fearless. He would be the leading scorer for the season. In his junior and senior year in high school, his coach didn't really play him, so he wasn't heavily drafted. He had better offers from other schools, but coach let me go meet Dan and his mom, Georgia, and see if I could make a difference. The minute Dan and I met, we hit it off. I flatfooted asked him to come, and without hesitation, he agreed. Dan and I would remain lifelong friends. Coach also recruited this kid that was seriously NBA material: six-foot-eight-inch Eric Smiley. The biggest challenge with Eric was that he had some legal baggage that seemed to follow him straight to OC. His girlfriend at that time was part of his problem, but he brought her along full time to OC. Eric had some fifty-point games with OC. He was awesome to watch develop as a player but that cloud just wouldn't leave him alone.

Coach got some other great talent in Nick Dennis, Brian Driskall, and Dan Jones's brother Rick Jones that gave us height, strength, aggression, and pure heart. Coach Sturgeon found guys with high basketball IQs and also knew how to be team players. In the first nineteen games of the season, we were scoring no less than 100 points per game. We went undefeated until we met Pierce Community College. With us, racking up all those wins and having one of the highest scoring team in the country for a junior college, we began to get national recognition. I think the attention made coach nervous because he started to change. He started coaching us differently.

One game, we played against a community college in Tacoma. We really should have beat this team on their home court, but we didn't. For some reason, this made coach extra pissed off because he didn't let us change out of our game uniforms after the game. Instead, he had us board the bus and head back to our gym. By the time we made it back to our gym, he had already called the local media and made us practice from 11:00 p.m. to 2:00 a.m. It was embarrassing, and it seemed pointless to everyone. Unfortunately, that wouldn't be the only time during the season that he did a stunt like that. When we traveled up to Canada for a game weekend and lost the game, he refused to give us our food money for the trip. This time, he made us go to the gym next to where we lost, and our women's basketball team was playing then had us run the court for two hours. We would also end up playing ten games in eleven days—the worst schedule of any college team. That season was tough, but the best outcome from the season was that as a team, we grew closer to each other. We all remained close even when some of us went our separate ways.

During our tough season, we went and watched a small division I school Warner Pacific College, which was a small Christian liberal arts college with an enrollment of about 1,400 students located in Portland, Oregon. When we watched Warner Pacific play, I watched how the coach interacted with his players, and he had a reputation for getting his players into the NBA. After our game, I knew I wanted to play for this coach. I went through the process of getting into the college, and Valarie ended up getting a scholarship to play both volleyball and softball there. It was tough saying goodbye to my teammates, but we were so close that everyone was supportive of my desire to move. Several of our OC players ended up, making transitions that would be a greater benefit to their college careers. I took a scholarship at Warner Pacific, and Brian Driskell would follow me there. Dan got a full-ride scholarship to Boise State, Rick left for Western Washington University to play football, Nick got married and had kids, while Eric ended up getting locked up for the same legal baggage he brought with him to OC.

CHAPTER 10

Valarie and I moved into a place in Portland so we could continue getting our education. I was ready to play ball until I found out that the coach that I wanted to play for took a position as head basketball coach at our sister school in Florida. I ended up playing for a coach that I am pretty sure didn't like, or at least didn't know how to coach African-American players. The new head basketball coach was Dan Dunn from Texas. Coach Dunn came to Warner Pacific with his wife and kids. He had three kids, one of whom was a quadriplegic. I felt confident he took the job because the environment in Portland, Oregon, would be better for his son.

Warner Pacific College was not an extremely diverse institution, so both Valarie and I struggled, making the adjustment. Bremerton wasn't super diverse either, but Warner Pacific made OC look like Atlanta. We stuck it out for two years at Warner Pacific even though Coach Dunn was affecting my game. No matter how much of a team player I tried to be, Coach Dunn would seemingly go out of his way to make sure I didn't get the playing time I deserved. The year I arrived, he recruited this white kid out of Oregon. He was a very smart kid and was very quiet. He played the point guard spot my first season at Warner. Now Brian had followed me from OC, and I knew how he played in the point guard spot. Not to take anything away from the kid from Oregon, but Brian was experienced and smart. He knew how to carry the team. But no matter how much this kid screwed up, Coach Dunn wouldn't take him out of the game.

In the two years I played at Warner, we only had two African Americans to play for him even though the school student population was 1,400. The two African-American players were me and

Anthony Cryer. Anthony was six feet two inches and from Seattle. As the only two on the team, we quickly bonded. Anthony was a lean point guard, but he could also play the shooting guard position. He was really smart and aggressive in his play. I loved playing with him because he made you play hard, and he feared no one.

There was one game where we played Multnomah Bible College at home. I had an amazing game. In the first half alone, I put thirty-two points on the board. For the entire second half, Coach Dunn took me out and sat me on the bench. The freshman from Oregon couldn't pay to get a bucket, and he was making error after error. Coach Dunn would not pull him out of the game, and I couldn't understand why. The next day, I went to see Coach Dunn in his office. I just needed to understand his reasoning for taking me out when I was having such a great game. When I asked him why he took me out, he told me I should have been happy because I had such a great game.

I snapped back and said, "I agree, but why take me out for having such a great game?"

He actually got upset and responded, "What did you want to do? Score forty points a night?"

I didn't get his logic. Of course, I wanted to score forty points a night. Who wouldn't want to have a forty-point-a-night game? I had to leave his office because that conversation was going to get much worse from there.

Afterward, every time I went to see him in his office, he would have me sit in a chair while he stood and talked over me. Of course, this dude was trying to show his power over me. Every time I confronted him and told him how I felt about how he was playing me, it never changed. He always played that power move and then keep everything on the court the same. I ended up talking to the athletic director for the school who saw everything this guy was doing on the court. At one point, the athletic director had words with him, and next thing I knew, the athletic director got transferred to another school, and Coach Dunn took over as the school's athletic director.

I wasn't the only player, having issues with the coach. Anthony Cryer felt the same way about how coach would let the white players do what they wanted while he and I were restricted in our playing time. Anthony eventually got so fed up with the way coach was handling the team that he quit the team. We knew the coach wasn't going to do anything, so I got some of the players to come talk to him and convinced him to come back to the team and finish out the season. I needed Anthony on the team with me. He was the player that pushed to you to play your hardest all the time. He was a smart player who deserved more respect from the coaching staff, but the best I could do was to give him as much respect as I could, and as a team, we could build the relationships we needed to be the best we could be in spite of the coach.

We both finished up, playing our senior year at Warner Pacific College. Anthony moved back to Seattle, and I left Warner Pacific College for Western Washington University. Since my college days playing basketball was over, I made good on a promise I made with Valarie. I promised that when basketball was over for me, we would go wherever she wanted to go. She liked Western Washington because it was far more diverse than Warner Pacific. Moving to Western Washington wouldn't change my ability to see little Marvin, and Andrea was amazingly flexible while I was in school, so Valarie and I moved. Going to school at Western Washington was a big change for me. Class sizes were a hundred students to one teacher while Warner Pacific and OC class size was ten to one. At Western Washington, I struggled because I no longer had direct access to the teachers. I could no longer get one-on-one help to make sure I was successful in class, but I pushed through.

I was still in love with playing basketball, so I started playing what they called noon basketball. Noon basketball was basically pickup games with old Western Washington student players. These were guys who were done playing for the college but still wanted to play. My dreams and passion for playing basketball beyond college was still on me. I seriously wanted to take my skills to the NBA, so I kept myself in shape until the time would come. I also took on a part-time job at night, working at AL's auto supply, working five nights a week to make sure my son had what he needed. In the middle of the day, I was playing noon basketball five days a week.

One day while playing noon ball, the Western Washington men's basketball coach came to the court to watch us play. Afterward, he approached me and suggested that I should try out for the professional basketball minor league. It was called the CBA, and at that time, Washington State had two teams. The coach just happened to have a friend who worked for one of the teams. He made a phone call, and I had a tryout that summer in Yakima Washington. The team was called the Yakima Sun Kings. As I was preparing for what could have been the next big thing for me in basketball, Valarie was preparing for her exit from my life. She told me she thought it would be best if we dated other people. By the end of our first year at Western Washington, we split up for good.

CHAPTER 11

Taking on a new chapter in my life, I embraced the possibilities of becoming a player in the NBA. I also thought what if this was a new opportunity for Andrea and I. Was there a possibility for the two of us to get back together and raise our son? Over the years in school, Ms. Philips and I talked about it. Every time Andrea and I were around each other, she could see the love we had for each other. She told me, "I know you are still in love with her." I tried not to give myself false hope, but we were both single, and maybe it was time to try again. We tried to reconnect for a whole two weeks, and we both figured out it was not going to work. Not because we didn't love each other. It was because we figured out we loved our friendship better. We loved and respected each other. We worked hard to show Marvin Jr. that we were united in loving him. Unlike the men in my family, I made it a point to kiss and hug my son as much as possible. I made sure I told him as often as possible that I loved him. Andrea let me be part of as many days in his life as I possibly could, but as for us being a couple, we knew we had grown beyond that. The best that we could both be for him was friends.

I started preparing for my summer tryout in Yakima, Washington, on the campus of Western Washington University. The men's basketball head coach who got me the tryout helped me out as much as he could with access to the gym and equipment for training. I continued playing noon basketball to keep my skills sharp. On some days, the assistant basketball coach for the women's team would come and join us for some of the noon basketball games. She had the respect of all of the guys, and she had some ball skills too. She was a basketball junkie like me, and she and I bonded over time, and we began dating. Her name was Cathy Crosslin.

Cathy grew up in Bellingham, Washington, and was the eldest of four kids to her parents. Her grandmother had married several rich men who died and left her their wealth. Needless to say, Cathy was also well off, but while she was dating me, her grandmother was very unhappy with her. Cathy's grandmother didn't like the fact that she was dating a black man. Her grandmother used her power over the family because during holidays or family gatherings, I could not be involved. Basically, I couldn't be seen. Cathy's dad and stepdad were awesome men. They were down-to-earth and genuine and didn't get caught up in using their wealth as a weapon. Cathy's stepdad was so wealthy, he ended up creating one of the most successful timeshare companies in the world. Even with his success, he was down-to-earth and friendly. Cathy loved sports and coaching but had a dream of one day becoming the head coach of a women's basketball team at a major university. Cathy and I dated for ten years, and over time, I got to know all of Cathy's family.

As the assistant coach of the Western Washington women's basketball team, she exceled. She was a great coach and could get her players to push themselves to levels of success they couldn't see in themselves. She understood how much to push a player to reach their best. With my tryouts coming up, she was the perfect person to help me get as prepared as possible. The tryout was open to players who wanted to play for the team in the upcoming basketball season. In order to tryout, each player had to pay a $250 nonrefundable fee, and they would only let forty players tryout per season. The tryout period was seven days of running drills and practicing set plays. The coaches observed how fast you learned because after spending the day practicing, they would separate players into two teams, watch you play the sets you learned earlier in the day, then they would cut players. They cut players until they got down to the top ten players. The ten players would be considered their all-star team. The selection of players that would eventually make it onto the team would come from the all-star team.

I was prepared for whatever this tryout was going to throw my way. I was in great shape, and I felt confident I could compete with anyone. I didn't know what the coaches were looking for, what size, type, of position they were looking for, but it didn't matter. If I could compete with the likes of Michael Jordan, Kenny Gattison, and the pure talent of the guys at the Rucker, I knew I could be ready. Cathy helped me get in the best shape both physically and mentally. I was ready!

When I arrived at the tryout, there were forty players. Of course, all of us were nervous because we didn't know what to expect but that was when preparation kicked in. As the tryouts progressed, all the nerves shook loose, and everyone was showcasing their skills. My tryouts were going great. Every day, the coaches were cutting players, but I kept on surviving the cut. At the end of the week, the coach's revealed their all-star team, and I made the cut. The next step was surviving the final all-star game because just before the game, the coaches revealed that they only needed a point guard and a shooting guard. I could play either position, so I felt great going into the final showcase.

The all-star game was full on talent. We put our all into the game. As a player fighting for a spot, we all wanted to stay in the game as long as we could. I got to stay on the floor the entire game. On one of the timeouts, one of the coach's assistants came over and told the coach that he needed to pick me for the team. At the end of the game, the coaches came over and congratulated me on such a great game. They told me they felt confident that I would make a great addition to the team. The only challenge would be if the NBA needed to send them a player that was drafted but not quite ready for prime time. I got the call that night. The NBA called and had a player that needed a little more development, so I didn't get a spot on the team.

I couldn't have done any more for that tryout. I showcased my skills and showed them the powerhouse player they could have had in me, but at the eleventh hour, all the stars didn't line up. I had to go home and regroup to see what was next. Of course, I would have loved to have been playing at that level and get the attention of the

NBA, but when I look back on that time, I was really proud of myself for making the all-star team. Being one of the top ten players at the tryout meant I was on the right track. I was only twenty-four years old. I still had time to make my dream a reality.

I had more than the other players, more motivation for pushing harder and someone to play for. My son was my prize whether I won or lost at the tryout. Marvin Jr. was two years old and didn't care if I got on the team. He cared that I was there, that I got to see his smiling face. He cared when I picked him up to observe how big he had gotten since the last time I saw him. Marvin Jr. was my pride and joy. No matter what went wrong in the world, he was always my bright and shining star. I wanted to be more for him and his mom, but I was so happy just to be in his presence, and he would give me fuel to keep pushing each day toward my dream.

Marvin Jr. was my fuel, and after spending time with him, I decided that it was time for me to keep tryout out, to get my education, and to keep hoping to get into the NBA so that I could make his life better. Succeeding in my classes at Western Washington was a struggle, so I transferred back to Warner Pacific in Portland, Oregon. Andrea and I worked it out so that Cathy would pick up Marvin Jr. when she would come down and visit me. She was still coaching the women's basketball team at Western Washington, so she had limited times when she could come down and visit me. Somehow, we worked it out, and in June of 1993, I graduated with my degree from Warner Pacific with Cathy in the audience and my son in my arms.

Graduating from college was a major accomplishment for me and my family. With my degree, I was the first person in my family to graduate from college. Cathy videotaped my graduation, which allowed my mom and dad to see me walk across the stage and receive my diploma. Not only did I receive my diploma, I shared my walk across the stage with my son. Having him in my arms highlighted the second greatest achievement in my life. The day my son came into this world was my first.

That moment was filled with so much gratitude. I was grateful to Cathy for her love, support, and pushing me to be the best version of me. She never missed a beat in her support of the things I wanted for me and my son's life. I was grateful to Andrea, not only for giving birth to my son, but also for allowing me to pursue my dreams and continuing to support me even when she didn't fully understand what I was doing, or why I was doing it. I was grateful to Ms. Phillips for continuing to be a voice of reason and a shoulder to cry on when I needed it. I was grateful to my mom and dad, my brothers, and sister. I was grateful for all of the support of friends I connected with along the journey. I was also grateful to basketball for being a friend for the ages, the one that was always there for me in one way or another.

After graduation, I stayed in Portland at Warner Pacific for about a year. During the year, I got the opportunity to play with some professional basketball players from the Portland Trailblazers. I played with Rod Strickland and Cliff Robinson at the University of Portland to keep myself sharp and in shape. We had some amazing games, and on one occasion, Rod and I were hanging out when he asked me why I wasn't playing on a professional level. I told him because I didn't have an agent to help me work the channels to get there. Rod made it a personal mission to connect me with a great agent. He ended up, connecting me with Houston Rockets player Robert Reed. Robert introduced me to his agent who connected me with John Lucas.

John Lucas was a former NBA player that hosted a summer USBL team in Houston, Texas. John Lucas had retired from the league and started a team that dealt with NBA players with drug and alcohol problems. The team was sponsored by the NBA, and most of the players that were allowed on the team were current NBA players, or who were on their last chance in the league. The NBA would send the players to John to see if there was any chance for them to recover from their addiction enough to get back onto an NBA team. John himself also struggled with drug addiction while he was playing in the NBA but figured out how to overcome it before it was too late. That was why the NBA was willing to support his program. Once a player completed all the program requirements, the players were allowed to return to the league. Part of his rehabilitation program was having the players play for his USBL team.

John gave me a chance to try out for his team, so Cathy and I worked out again to get me in the best physical and mental shape.

This was my nine-to-five job, working out and preparing me for what I saw as my opportunity to make my dream a reality. If John saw my potential and made a phone call, I could be in the NBA. At the time of my tryouts, John had four open positions. I knew the process for the tryout: a week-long showcase with cuts every day. They would cut players every day until there were just ten players. There was also some politics involved. If the coaching staff member took you out of the game to talk to you, that was an indication that you had a better chance of being selected. There were eighty guys trying out for the four spots, and I was getting picked up by the coaches for dinner and socializing.

The final day of the tryouts, I was chosen to be one of the top ten players in the camp. This meant I would have the opportunity to play in the all-star game, which was the final exhibition at the camp. The all-star games was a hell of a game with current NBA players, semipro players, trying to get into the NBA, and me. Just after the game, I was told I got in. I was going to Florida for the final tryout on John's team. I made it. I did everything I needed to do. I could make a better life for my son. I left that camp and made a bee line to the hotel where Cathy and my son were staying. I could share the exciting news with them: I made the final cut. All of the hard work and sacrifices I made led me to this moment.

Later that night, after we all settled into the excitement of the moment, I got a devastating call. One of the coaches called me and told me that John got a call from the NBA, and they had a player, a guy that they needed to send him that would take my spot. John only had four spots to fill based on position. The position I was selected to fill, point guard, would now be taken by this guy, and I was out.

In that second, following the shock of the announcement that my dreams of playing in the NBA were dashed again, I quit trying. In that moment, I decided it was time to do something else. I was twenty-six years old, I was too old to keep this up, and I couldn't bear the disappointment again. I kept myself together long enough to get Marvin Jr. to Andrea. After that, I felt like I traveled to hell. All I knew was an all-consuming depression.

CHAPTER 12

H ow can a person work so hard at one thing and not be successful at it? How is it that passion for one thing in your life does not drive you to your ultimate success? Isn't passion the driving force to success? At the moment the passion of my life stopped seeking me, I stopped playing it. I spent the next two weeks in a deep depression. I was hurt and confused. This thing I put my absolute all into failed me. I spent the next two weeks, pouring my hurt, confusion, and hopelessness into a glass and drinking it away.

I drank two to three forty-ounce beers daily. That was my medicine to help me process what the hell was going on. I was fighting the idea that my dreams were going. I worked my ass off, and I was in the best shape of my life. I stayed focused on what I wanted, and I went for it. I had a goal. I was going to create a way to support my son better than anyone else I had ever seen. I would help Andrea and her family come up. My passion would finally start paying me back for all of the blood, sweat, and tears I gave to it.

What made the depression so difficult was in my mind, I still never had it in my mind that I wouldn't make it. I never saw that I couldn't make it. I held onto the idea that it was just a matter of time before I made it, and I kept inching closer and closer to it. I just couldn't make sense of it. Drinking didn't necessary help me forget, or get over it. It just gave me a temporary relief to numb myself to the pain, stress, disappointment, and anger that crowded around me when I got the call that the dream was now dead.

I traded in playing basketball for drinking. I started drinking so heavily that Cathy got worried about me. There was barely a time when I didn't have a drink in my hand. Fortunately, because Cathy and I were moving to a place closer to SeaTac Airport so Marvin Jr. wasn't around to see me, Cathy got up the courage to confront me about my drinking. She asked me to stop drinking and go back to basketball. By the time she confronted me about my drinking, I had come to the realization that it wasn't meant for me to be a professional basketball player. It hurt like hell to admit that to myself, but I had to come to that crossroad.

I didn't stop drinking. I mean I heard Cathy asking me to stop, but what was I going to replace the drinking with? The pain and the hurt weren't any less, so I continued to need my medicine in a bottle. After about a month, it was time to get back to be a sensible parent. Marvin Jr. was coming back around, and there was no way I wanted him to see me that way. I also had to figure out how I was going to make money to take care of him.

Cathy took a girl's high school basketball head coaching job in Bellevue, Washington. She asked me to be her assistant coach. In my heart, I was not feeling coaching because I hadn't given up being a player. There is a transition period that has to happen when you are changing up your passion. But I didn't have any other options on the table, so I told her I would give it a try, and my effort made her happy.

My very first day of coaching girls' high school basketball, two players walked into the gym crying.

Cathy walked up to me after seeing them cry and asked me, "What did you do?" This was a great start, I wasn't even close to them girls. I couldn't have done anything if I tried.

I told Cathy, "Nothing!"

Cathy went over to the girls and asked them what happened. The girls told her they got a B in their class. Fortunately, it got better, not worse, as it related to Cathy and I coaching together.

We started out, coaching the Bellevue High School girls' basketball team for three years. Coming out of my depression, coaching turned out to be a life saver. I would have never thought about it if she hadn't presented it to me. It finally dawned on me when I was working with the girls at Bellevue High School and seeing how they were developing that I could coach basketball and that I enjoyed it. Coaching brought me same joy as playing as if I were out on the court, playing ball with the girls myself. I had to learn that I could still love basketball while coaching. I could love basketball for more than what I needed it to give me. Basketball was a relationship no different than being married, or any other intimate relationship. I was married to basketball.

Once I got into the rhythm of coaching, I started focusing on teaching my son all that I was teaching the girls. In my opinion, after working with these girls, females are tougher than the men. I loved coaching girls because their pain and endurance thresholds are much higher than boys. Once they are loyal to you, they are loyal to you. They don't care about nothing but the basketball. With boys, it's all about "Me! Me! Me!"

We had a great group of girls, playing basketball those years, and we had major success.

We had so much success that we caught the eye of Jim Webster, an investment banker who loved basketball and started an AAU girls' basketball program called the Seattle Magic. The program was a national program that placed elite female basketball players into a position to get into college and receive scholarships. Jim started the program because his daughter Karen didn't receive great coaching, nor the visibility he thought she deserved while she played basketball in high school. Jim was very excited to have me and Cathy in the program, which had about 325 kids, participating and a program budget for the summer of about $50,000.

Cathy, Jim, and I met for breakfast every Saturday morning at his favorite café in Bellevue. For ten summers, we coached in the Seattle Magic program. We became family with Jim, his wife, and four kids. We watched his daughter Karen excel in basketball in high school and go on to play four years at UNLV. After ten years of watching Jim build and run this amazing program, Jim committed suicide. He took a shot gun to his family's second home and shot himself.

Jim was an amazing guy. Not only did he build an incredible opportunity for female basketball players to get the attention they deserved in order to go to college and play basketball, he also built a great family where he knew everyone's name, background, and coaching abilities. He gave hope to kids when others may not have given them a chance. He put some young basketball stars into some big schools where their light could really shine. Jim motivated and inspired me in indescribable ways. His death really broke my heart. I really loved and respected him. His suicide was so hard for me to accept because whenever I saw him, he was happy and upbeat. But that is the way it is with depression: out in public, you put on the face you want everyone to see and come home and suffer in silence. He will be sadly missed by me and many others.

After Jim died, coaching changed from me. I began to think more about my future and my son's, and it was during this time, I began to focus more on making sure he had a better future. I had been taking Marvin Jr. to all of the Seattle Magic practices. While coaching the girls, I would have him out on the floor, teaching him how to play the game. He learned how to handle the basketball at the age of ten from Sheila Lambert, one of the Seattle Magic players Jim Webster took a serious interest in. Sheila would go on to break every high school scoring record, not just the girls' basketball records but the boys' as well. Sheila would also go on to become not only one of Baylor Universities women's basketball best players but was also picked number seven in the 2002 WNBA draft for the Detroit Shock.

By the time Marvin Jr. was about thirteen years old, he had spent time being a junior coach with me and Cathy. Marvin Jr. would sit on the bench and watch the game. When the girls made an error, or didn't do what we instructed them, Marvin Jr. would be the first person, coming over, asking why they did or did not do something they were told to do. Cathy once said in an article that Marvin Jr. had a coach's mind. "He would know what I was going to say even before I said it." I saw that Marvin Jr. already had a high basketball IQ in junior high. It was time for me to help guide him one on one when we weren't coaching. I decided if I was going to give him more of me, I needed to get my act together financially. I took a job as a manager trainee at a sporting goods store in Silverdale, Washington.

CHAPTER 13

New Year's Eve, 2000. Andrea, her fiancé, and I decided to go to a local night club to bring in the New Year. We went to a club where one of my longtime friends worked as a bouncer. His day job was working for the county, helping kids. He and I sat at the front of the club, catching up. Andrea and her fiancé went into the club to dance. Before we entered the club, there was a high-speed car chase with the Bremerton Police Department. The young man they were chasing they would later catch, but at that time we entered the club, there was a lot of police activity across the street from the club. About four hours later, Andrea and her fiancé came up to the front of the club, and we decided to leave. The police activity was still high, but with the high-speed car chase and the fact that it was New Year's Eve, the amount of police made sense. Andrea and her fiancé got into their car, and I climbed into mine alone. We both decided we would stay out of the police's way. Andrea and her fiancé turned right down the hill away from the club while I turned left going down the hill. Both turns would keep us away from the police who were at the gas station across the street from the club. When I made the left turn out of the parking lot, there was another police officer, sitting in the parking lot of the local gas station to the left of the nightclub.

The police officer motioned for me to pull over, and I did without an issue. I rolled down my window, and when the officer came to my window, I asked him why he stopped me. The officer did not answer my question and, instead, asked me if I had been drinking. I told him I had not been drinking and then asked again why he stopped me. He explained that he pulled me over because my music was too loud. He explained that there was a noise ordinance in the city. Note that I was being stopped on New Year's Eve. There was constant stream of fireworks, going off at that time. I told the officer that I would turn the music down, but before I could reach for the volume dial, the officer reached in through my window and turned off my car. I told him that I would have turned the car off myself if he had asked, but he responded with force for me to get out of the car. I was so confused. I had no idea why the officer was coming at me that way.

The officer tried to pull me out of the car, and at this point, I knew this encounter was not going to end well. When I got out of the car, I took off, running for the phone booth that was on the gas station lot. I wanted to call Andrea to let her know what was going on and to come back quickly to get me. When I got to the phone booth, two officers grabbed me and pulled me out of the phone booth. I made up my mind. I wasn't going to cooperate with these guys and began fighting them for my life. The officers sprayed me with mace, threw me to the ground, and punched me so hard, they knocked me out. By the time I woke up, I had blood everywhere as I sat handcuffed and in jail.

The news media put out stories about my arrest and completely damaged my reputation. My son was embarrassed and teased at school by kids who had heard about my arrest. I finally got to call my son from the jail, and I explained everything that had happened. It was so painful to put my son through that embarrassment, but I assured him I was all right. After about three days, Ms. Phillips and Cathy posted my bail, which was set at $20,000. I was fired from my management position at Big 5 Sporting Goods because I couldn't report to work because I was in jail. When I did get released, no one wanted to hire me because of the reports in the media made me out to be a monster. I finally got a job from the athletic director at Olympic College, coaching the women's basketball team.

This was a very tough time for me because only the people who knew me well believed that I had not done what I was accused of. Those who knew me supported me in ways I could not have expected. My longtime friend Clark Whitney, a local certified public accountant, and my pastor Bishop Robinson of Emmanuel Apostolic Church in Bremerton started a campaign in and around the city to clear my name. They had lived in Bremerton for many, many years and knew the issues what people of color were facing with the Bremerton Police Department. These two guys demanded an audience with the chief of police on my behalf to find out the truth about my arrest. In the midst of finding out the truth, the courts issued a court date for me, and the public defender told me that I could face up to seven years in prison for third degree assault of two officers. If I were to go to prison, I would lose my right to vote, my right to carry a firearm, and the respect of my son who wouldn't see his father for seven years.

Cathy and I decided with was time to get me an attorney. The attorney could not be from the local community because everyone seemed determined to believe the police department. We hired a badass attorney from Seattle who was well versed in the misconduct of police officers. His first step was to hire a private investigator whose job was to look into the Bremerton Police Department officers' conduct. After the attorney received the report from the private investigator, he told us that we had a really strong case, but it would cost another $20,000. Cathy and I raised the money and hired the attorney for my case. The prosecuting attorney tried to get us to accept that they would reduce the charges, but in doing so, the police department would not have to admit fault nor pay any damages. We took the case to trial.

The trial went on for about a week, and both Clark Whitney and Bishop Robinson were called to testify on my behalf. Clark's emotional plea on the witness stand almost got him charged with contempt. He used his time on the stand to voice his outrage about how his taxpayer dollars were being spent on this ridiculous trial. By the time the week-long trial was over, I was acquitted of all charges, and the jury asked to speak with me personally after the trial was over. As the judge was sharing the request of the jurors, he explained that in his twenty years on the bench, no jury had asked to speak with the defendant personally.

I met with the jurors, and it was one of the most loving and caring group of people I had ever met. The jurors were outraged at the behavior of the police officers. The jurors told me that if I opted to file suit against the Bremerton Police Department that every one of them would testify on my behalf. I sued the Bremerton Police Department and won. It took a year to complete the lawsuit, but in the end, my reputation was restored. I had my freedom, and my son got to see what justice really looked like.

While the lawsuit was going on, Marvin Jr. was developing into a basketball powerhouse. He had reached the status of one of the top high school basketball players in the country. A friend of mine, Craig Murray, was running an AAU program and had been asking me to let Marvin Jr. attend the University of Kansas Basketball camp. Marvin Jr. was only fifteen, and I really wanted him to stay close to home. After considering what opportunities I could be holding Marvin Jr. back from, I agreed to let him go to the camp with Craig. Craig was friends with the former University of Kansas and NBA player Danny Manning. Danny heard how amazing Marvin Jr. was along with the fact that he was six feet five inches at the time that he went and talked to legendary coach Roya Williams about Marvin Jr. Once Marvin Jr. arrived at the camp, Roy Williams thought, *At fifteen years old, Marvin Jr. was too advanced for the camp participants and instead had him participate in his night camps with more advanced players.*

Roy and Danny saw the potential right away and started sending Marvin Jr. scholarship offers. During this time, I also decided to put Marvin Jr. into an elite AAU program based in Seattle, which would turn out to be one of the best programs in the country. Marvin Jr. got to be exposed to some of the best players in the country and would end up, playing well against the likes of LeBron James, Dwight Howard, Josh Smith, and Al Jefferson all of whom would go on to be first-round draft picks in the NBA. Marvin Jr.'s basketball career really exploded when he was a junior in high school. He played in the Reebok classic in Las Vegas, Nevada. Marvin Jr. scored forty points against Dwight Howard and Josh Smith's AAU team called the Atlanta Celtics. The Atlanta Celtics were loaded with division I talent. Marvin Jr. scored forty points against them and fouled out of the game. As Marvin Jr. was leaving the game, a packed house crowd gave him a standing ovation. Roy Williams from Kansas watched Marvin Jr.'s behavior after he had to sit down. Roy watched as Marvin Jr. handed water to his teammates and made sure they had towels. When most other kids would have been sitting on the sidelines with an attitude and angry, here was Marvin Jr., being a real teammate. Marvin Jr.'s attitude and behavior on top of his basketball skills made Roy want to recruit him for his program.

In 2001, during a break from summer basketball, one of my dreams for my son came true. I got the opportunity to take fifteen-year-old Marvin Jr. back home to my home Wallace, North Carolina. For the first time in his life, he was able to meet my mom and dad. Marvin Jr. had developed a great relationship over the phone with his grandparents, but for the first time, they could love and hug on the grandson they kept clippings on and watched on television whenever possible. The moment my parents saw him, they fell in love. My mom more than everyone else because she didn't even want anyone get near him or talk to him. She became super territorial even with me. I wanted to take Marvin Jr. to go play basketball where I played as a kid, and Mom said, "No!" She went a step further and told me, his father, to leave him alone. She said, "Let him enjoy and relax with me." I knew she loved him and wanted to spend as much time as possible with him. While in Wallace, Marvin Jr. always carried his basketball with him. One night, he tried to sleep with it in his bed. My mother stepped in and told him, "Baby, I love you, but you can't take the ball to bed with you." Marvin Jr., being the respectful person he is, honored his grandma and slept without the basketball that night.

It was amazing, watching my mother interact with Marvin Jr. She was so attentive and loving, but I noticed that since my last visit, my mother had lost even more weight. The previous visit, before Marvin Jr. came down, I remember asking my mother why she had lost so much weight. Mom shrugged off my questions and told me she just had an ulcer. On this trip, I pressed a little harder because it was hard to believe an ulcer was making her grow frail. Finally, Mom explained that ten years earlier, she was in a car accident with my brother Bradford. The accident was so bad that both she and my brother had to be rushed to the hospital. While they were examining her, they found a small mass in her stomach and advised her to get it checked out. Mom never got it checked out, and it evolved into pancreatic cancer.

In 2002, one year after meeting Marvin Jr. face to face, Mom passed away from cancer. He never got to see her again, and she never got to see him play. It was hard on us both, but I think it took wind out of Marvin Jr. as it seemed he stayed very emotional about her passing for quite a long time. Having basketball was a great way to process hard times.

The summer of his junior year of high school was amazing. Marvin Jr. not only became one of the top-ranked players in the nation along with players like Al Jefferson, Dwight Howard, Shawn Livingston, and Josh Smith, he was also becoming one of the top three high school forwards in the country. He was being to be recruited by every major college in the country like Kansas, Kentucky, UCLA, Florida, the University of North Carolina, Wake Forest, University of Washington, and Gonzaga to name a few. I would come to his house daily and see bags and bags of letters from all these different schools. He received so many letters that he began to paste them on the walls all over his room until every space was covered even the ceiling. With so many offers in his junior year, he decided that it would be best to wait and see what his senior year would bring.

Going into his senior year, Marvin Jr. was six feet seven inches and starting to attract NBA scouts. The scouts would come visit Bremerton during the summer just to watch him play. I had been forced to go back and work for Big 5 Sporting Goods after I was acquitted of all charges, but when the scouts started, I knew I needed some other place to work without the cloud of my case, lingering every time I stepped into the store. I got a job as a manager at Enterprise Rental Car, and it gave me the flexibility I needed to be there for my son and support him financially as well.

Marvin Jr.'s senior year got really stressful for him with everyone, asking him what he was going to do after leaving high school. Would he pick a college and continue his development, or skip school and enter the NBA draft? We came together as a family. We wanted to make sure that whatever happened, Marvin Jr. was satisfied with his choice. Marvin Jr., Andrea, and I agreed that we would work together each week and narrow down his choice until we got down to his top five schools. In the meantime, his high school coach and I would coordinate open gym for the college coaches to fly into Bremerton and watch him play in open gym. Every major college you could think of came to the open gym time, the most persistent being Coach Roy Williams. Coach Williams was still at the University of Kansas at the beginning of Marvin Jr.'s senior year. By the middle of the year, Coach Williams left Kansas and took the head coaching job at the University of North Carolina.

CHAPTER 14

Throughout the years, whether I was playing at OC, Warner Pacific, or the noon basketball games at Western Washington, when I was coaching the girls in college, or high school, when I spent ten years, coaching AAU, or hanging out with all of the lifelong friends I have made in and around my passionate love for basketball, I was fortunate that I could have my son with me. From the time he was born, he has been around basketball, and I always embraced the opportunity to pour anything that I learned into him. The definition of a dad for me. I was basketball, and I poured it into my son because that was the skill set I had. And when I spent time with my son, I gave him what I had, which was basketball.

Many people would misconstrue our relationship as me, managing him, or grooming his basketball career more than building a relationship with him. Basketball was our secondary gig. We had our moments where we would have our private conversations, those conversations where you don't want anyone else to hear. That was our time. People actually want to make it seem that I was always on him, and I was making him do this or that, like I was spearheading him into the NBA, which wasn't even close to the picture. My whole goal with Marvin Jr. was to make him a good high school basketball player. I truthfully didn't have a clue that he would go to Carolina because I didn't know how tall he was going to be. I knew if I taught him these skills sets, it would get him through high school. I felt good because I was doing something great for my son. I was also building a relationship with him. I have heard some people talking, or while I was in an interview, looking at their computer, they would have, "You need to be more concerned about being his dad than his manager." Those people don't get it. Being a father is about pouring you into your child. All the gifts and talents you have so they don't have to start from scratch. That was what I always prayed I would do for him.

In the summer of 2004, Marvin Jr. announced he would be attending the University of North Carolina with Coach Roy Williams. Coach Williams had been, in my opinion, Marvin's biggest fan. He would fly in weekly, texted him daily, and even brought his wife on her first ever recruiting trip to see Marvin Jr. play. What I loved about him was his honesty during his visit. He never once told my son he would immediately put him in the starting lineup. His only promise was that if Marvin Jr. joined the team, UNC would win a national championship. We believed him, and he made good on that promise.

When we learned that Andrea needed back surgery in 2005, Marvin, Jr. put his hat into the NBA draft and was picked second overall in the 2005 draft, playing for the Atlanta Hawks. Since 2005, Marvin, Jr. has made me extremely proud. He is an amazing player, father, friend, and man. He has held his head high and taught me that love conquers all. Love conquers all the pains of the past, the effects of our environment, and the transitions we must make when the passions of our heart make a turn we are not expecting.

On October 29, 2014, after nine years in the NBA, Marvin Jr. started his first game as a Charlotte Hornet. The Charlotte Hornets are owned by Michael Jordan. It's incredible to know that sometimes when you think you are chasing a passion, that passion is chasing you. Everywhere I turned in my life, basketball was there. Every time I came to a crossroad, basketball was there. Every time I lost, loved, or lived; basketball was there. Our passions are our guides, and if you let them, they will define the split seconds in our lives. They will give meaning and understanding to this crazy experiment called life.

One thing I know for certain, so far in this life. I love you, Son.

EPILOGUE

In 2006, my dad died from prostate cancer. I was with him on the day he died. It was late at night, and Dad and I were the only two awake. The house was full of family and loved ones, but they were asleep, and I got to steal away a moment with just my dad and I. Dad and I just enjoyed each other's presence and talked throughout our time together. At one point, just before it was his time to go home, Dad turned to me and told me, "Son, don't you let nobody worry you. You did all right by me!"

That affirmation meant I finally got the love I was looking for from him. A lifetime of fighting for the love I couldn't explain I needed. It was a moment that captured all that I poured into loving my son. Likely why I love all my sons Marvin, Demetrius, J'Tonn, and Juwan the way I do.

My dad was proud of the man I had become. He was proud of the decisions I made along this journey. Hearing that from him laid to rest many of the anxieties and fears I had. It allowed me to lay him to rest in true peace with nothing unspoken.

During the last years of my dad's life, I believe he got to enjoy himself. After he learned about his cancer diagnosis, he got the opportunity to see Marvin Jr. play basketball. He even got a special seat at UNC-Chapel Hill Arena, given to him by the late great "Dean Smith." Because of Marvin Jr., coach told him he could sit in anywhere in the basketball arena, which he chose to sit directly behind the players.

When Marvin Jr. was still playing for the Atlanta Hawks, Dad came to stay with me in Atlanta and got to sit and watch his grandson play professional basketball. I believe those are the priceless moments that we must cherish. For life is not promised, but the promise of living is available for all.

Marvin Williams Sr. was a member of the US Navy from 1983 to 1989. He also is a current member of The Fathers and Men of Professional Basketball Players organization, a group dedicated to improving fathers' and families' relationships and providing financial assistance and mentorship to families in need. He has also been featured on TNT Sports, CBS Sports, and FOX Sports Southeast. He has also been a guest speaker at The Tom Joyner Family Reunion. Marvin has also coached basketball for over thirty years, which includes high school and college. He currently resides in Charlotte, North Carolina, with his son and two granddaughters.

CPSIA information can be obtained
at www.ICGtesting.com
Printed in the USA
JSHW050120130920
7833JS00001B/40

9 781646 541249